DNS and BIND Cookbook

DNS and BIND Cookbook

Cricket Liu

O'REILLY®

Beijing · Cambridge · Farnham · Köln · Paris · Sebastopol · Taipei · Tokyo

DNS and BIND Cookbook
by Cricket Liu

Published by O'Reilly & Associates, Inc., 1005 Gravenstein Highway North, Sebastopol, CA 95472.

O'Reilly & Associates books may be purchased for educational, business, or sales promotional use. Online editions are also available for most titles (*safari.oreilly.com*). For more information, contact our corporate/institutional sales department: (800) 998-9938 or *corporate@oreilly.com*.

Editor:	Mike Loukides
Production Editor:	Colleen Gorman
Cover Designer:	Ellie Volckhausen
Interior Designer:	David Futato

Printing History:

October 2002:	First Edition.

ISBN: 0-596-00410-9
[M]

Table of Contents

Preface

I'm a pretty good casual Scrabble® player. Not a great one, mind you, but good enough so that close friends and family don't much like playing with me. (My sister claims that *she* doesn't like to play with me because I always cheated when we played games as kids, but I have no recollection of that.) I have a decent-sized vocabulary, I'm a good speller, and I've been doing the New York Times Crossword since I worked at HP and my manager, Lee, taught me the basics, so I now know all kinds of otherwise-useless crossword-puzzle words. But I'm still far from a great player.

A friend of mine, who's among the brightest people I know, told me about a friend of his who's a top competitive Scrabble player. He'd never played him before, so he challenged him to a game one day. On his second turn, my friend had six common letters in his rack, UDINTS, plus the blank (which, for those of you uninitiated in the ways of Scrabble, can be used as any letter). He was sure there were plays that would let him bingo—play all seven of his letters and earn a coveted 50 point bonus.

He told his opponent as much, who replied, "Well, let me see!" After looking over the tiles for a moment, he said, "Oh, yeah, there are at least 15 bingos there." Somewhat incredulously, my friend said, "Yeah, right. What are they?" To which his opponent replied, "You could make your blank any of AEFILMQRGNU, and make any of the following across the E:

Making it an "A": AUDIENTS
Making it an "E": DETINUES
Making it an "F": UNSIFTED
Making it an "I": NUDITIES, DISUNITE, or UNTIDIES
Making it an "L": UNLISTED, INSULTED, or DILUENTS
Making it an "M": MISTUNED
Making it a "Q": SQUINTED
Making it an "R": INTRUDES
Making it an "G": DUNGIEST
Making it an "N": DUNNITES
Making it a "U": UNSUITED

Now, this guy wasn't so quick with anagrams that he came up with all of these on the fly. No, he knew a Scrabble mnemonic device—a recipe, if you will—for remembering them all: finding the anagram DUNNITES, he remembered the magic sentence "A fire quelling material," any of whose letters can be added to UDINTS and E to make a bingo. Of course, he *did* have to come up with the anagrams of each combination of letters, which is no mean feat. (Dunnite, ironically, is the name of a high explosive—not exactly the stuff to be smothering the ol' campfire with.)

You'd think that all you'd need to play a wicked game of Scrabble is an outsized vocabulary, but there's much more to it than that. To become a competitive Scrabble player, you need to devote hundreds of hours to memorization: all of the English words you can spell with a "Q" but no "U"; all the two-letter words; all the three-letter words.* In my brain, too much valuable space is wasted remembering which country the ccTLD *fm* belongs to (the Federated States of Micronesia, and I swear I didn't have to look it up) to commit stuff like that to memory.

Now, many name server administrators have a good grasp of the basics of DNS theory and name server configuration—they're fluent. But to be a complete administrator, you also need a set of commonly (and not-so-commonly) used BIND configurations. Then, when the occasion arises, you can bingo and impress the boss. Or go home early. Whichever.

Unlike Scrabble players, you don't need to hold all this in your head. I often pop open *DNS and BIND* (O'Reilly & Associates) to check the syntax of some less-common *named.conf* substatements, so I certainly don't expect everyone to remember all of the nuances of BIND configuration. And while I think *DNS and BIND* is a good book for learning about DNS theory and BIND configuration, I must admit it's somewhat less useful as a reference than as a tutorial. Sometimes you just don't feel up to slogging through a whole chapter to figure out how to set up classless *in-addr. arpa* delegation, and you can't find the answer you're looking for in the relevant mailing lists—or you're uncertain of the answer you do find.

This book is designed to "round you out" as a name server administrator by showing you just what you can do with BIND and how to do it, from the straightforward (the 10 English words with a "Q" but no "U") to the intricate (all the bingos you can make with SATINE plus a blank).

This book expressly *doesn't* concentrate on DNS theory. For that, I'd (not surprisingly) recommend *DNS and BIND*. Without an understanding of the theory behind DNS, you're like the Southeast Asian Scrabble players who memorize the spelling—but not the meaning or pronunciation—of tens of thousands of English words: all syntax, no semantics.

---

* For a fascinating account of the process of becoming a competitive Scrabble player, see Stefan Fatsis's excellent book, *Word Freak*.

As in other O'Reilly Cookbooks, the chapters in this book begin with simpler recipes and progress toward the more complex. The simpler recipes should be useful to anyone with a basic knowledge of DNS, while the more advanced may come in handy to even seasoned hostmasters. Each recipe starts with an explanation of a problem and a concise solution to that problem, followed by a more detailed explanation of the solution and, often, variations. At the end, you'll find references to other, related recipes and more complete coverage of the topics in *DNS and BIND* and elsewhere.

Platform and Version

This book covers both BIND 8 and 9 name servers. The latest versions of these name servers as of this book's publication were 8.3.3 and 9.2.1. Thanks to the availability of early snapshots of BIND 9.3.0, I've been able to include a few peeks at its features.

When a feature I've described is only available in a particular version of BIND, I've tried to note that in the recipe. In general, however, I'd recommend running the latest released version of BIND 8 or 9.

I run my name servers on FreeBSD (currently the 4.5 release), so many of the examples are drawn from that operating system.

Organization

Chapter 1, *Getting Started*, covers what you need to know to get started with a BIND name server: downloading and compiling BIND, registering a new domain name and configuring a name server. Chapter 2, *Zone Data*, describes how to create a zone data file and add records to it. Chapter 3, *BIND Name Server Configuration*, covers configuring BIND 8 and 9 name servers, from setting a name server's working directory to serving multiple views of a single zone.

Chapter 4, *Electronic Mail*, describes how to set up email destinations, while Chapter 5, *BIND Name Server Operations*, covers topics in name server control and management. Chapter 6, *Delegation and Registration*, describes both how to establish and police delegation from your zone to its subzones, and how to manage the delegation to your zone from its parent.

The last five chapters deal with more specialized topics. Chapter 7, *Security*, contains recipes on securing your name server against various types of attacks. Chapter 8, *Interoperability and Upgrading*, describes the pitfalls of running multiple versions of BIND name servers or heterogeneous name server environments, and warns of gotchas when upgrading from one version of BIND to another. Chapter 9, *Resolvers and Programming*, describes both basic resolver configuration and simple resolver programming using Perl's Net::DNS module. Chapter 10, *Logging and Troubleshooting*, provides troubleshooting tips. Finally, Chapter 11, *IPv6*, covers

IPv6: setting up a name server to respond to IPv6-based queries, and handling the forward- and reverse-mapping of hosts with IPv6 addresses.

Audience

This book is intended primarily for system and network administrators who manage zones and one or more BIND name servers. However, the recipes in certain chapters may be of interest to a broader audience:

- Postmasters working with DNS may benefit from the recipes in Chapter 4.
- Programmers (particularly Perl programmers) may find the recipes in the second half of Chapter 9 useful for learning how to send DNS queries and updates.

Other Books and Resources

Many of the recipes in this book include references to other books and a few web-based resources. Here's a list of those:

Apache, The Definitive Guide, Peter Laurie and Ben Laurie (O'Reilly & Associates)
> For coverage of how to configure virtual hosts in Apache.

The BIND 9 Administrator Reference Manual, the Nominum BIND Development Team; the Internet Software Consortium (*http://www.nominum.com/resources/ documentation/Bv9ARM.pdf*)
> Nicknames "the ARM," this is the standard configuration reference for BIND 9 name servers, invaluable for name server administrators.

DNS and BIND, by Paul Albitz and Cricket Liu (O'Reilly)
> Textbook-style coverage of the Domain Name System and its BIND implementation, organized to follow the maturation of an administrator.

DNS on Windows 2000, by Matt Larson and Cricket Liu (O'Reilly)
> A special edition of *DNS and BIND* that substitutes the Microsoft DNS Server for the BIND name server.

Conventions Used in This Book

The following typographic conventions are used in this book:

Italic
> Used for filenames, directories, domain names, variables, and URLs.

Constant Width
> Used for code examples.

Constant Width Italic
> Used to indicate replaceables in examples.

This book uses one terminological convention that merits special note. There are many BIND configuration substatements that you can use within several different statements. For example, you can specify *allow-transfer* within a *zone* statement, within an *options* statement, and within a *view* statement. When I'm referring only to the first use, I call it the *allow-transfer zone* substatement. When referring to any of the three, I just call it the *allow-transfer* substatement. While I'm not sure this convention is common, it seemed like a natural, compact way of expressing the idea.

Comments and Questions

Please address comments and questions concerning this book to the publisher:

O'Reilly & Associates, Inc.
1005 Gravenstein Highway North
Sebastopol, CA 95472
(800) 998-9938 (in the United States or Canada)
(707) 829-0515 (international or local)
(707) 829-0104 (fax)

We have a web page for this book, where we list errata, examples, or any additional information. You can access this page at:

http://www.oreilly.com/catalog/dnsbindckbk/

To comment or ask technical questions about this book, send email to:

bookquestions@oreilly.com

For more information about our books, conferences, Resource Centers, and the O'Reilly Network, see our web site at:

http://www.oreilly.com

Acknowledgments

First, I'd like to thank this book's reviewers, Robbie Allen, Nate Campi and Jay Kreibich, whose close reading of the text caught more errors than I'd like to admit to, and whose suggestions improved nearly every recipe. I'd also like to thank the Internet Software Consortium and Nominum, for their hard work on the development of BIND 8 and 9, without which I imagine my career would have veered in a wildly different direction.

While I'm up on this podium, let me acknowledge the unsung heroes of the BIND Users and BIND 9 Users mailing lists, who do a tremendous job of answering dozens of DNS and BIND questions each week—some of them for the nth time. I hope this book helps alleviate their workload a little. Who knows? Maybe we'll be able to use it like the longtime regulars in the bar, telling each other jokes by calling out each joke's number: "How do I point my domain name at a particular URL?" "Recipe 2.6!"*

I'm grateful to my friend Paul Phillips, for the use of his Scrabble anecdote, and for his occasional—but always entertaining—dispatches from the world of professional poker. And I am, as ever, indebted to my friend Paul Albitz, under whose wing I got my start, and who sets a sterling example as a patient teacher, selfless coauthor and methodical engineer.

The folks at O'Reilly, as always, have been wonderful to work with, especially my editor, Mike Loukides.

Finally, my love and thanks to my family: to my mom, my first reviewer, whose voice you undoubtedly hear in my writing; to my dad, for hours of academic tutelage; to my sister ("You shut up!") for her good humor; and of course to my wife, Paige, and son, Walt, and my dogs, Dakota and Annie, for their love and for lost hours.

* For a variation on this joke, see *http://www.awpi.com/Combs/Shaggy/929.html*.

## CHAPTER 1

Getting Started

1.0   Introduction

All first moves in a Scrabble game have a few things in common: you play across the star, the opening square. You try to score high without opening up a premium square, particularly a Triple Word Score, for your opponent.

Most DNS setups start in very similar ways, too: you register a new domain and maybe a reverse-mapping domain; choose a version of BIND; download the BIND source code, if you need to, and build it; configure a primary master and slave name server; and make sure both name servers start at boot time.

This chapter will guide you through those opening moves and help you get your DNS infrastructure established.

1.1   Finding More Information
About DNS and BIND

Problem

You can't find information you need about the Domain Name System or BIND in this book.

Solution

For much more complete coverage of DNS theory and a step-by-step approach to setting up BIND name servers, pick up a copy of *DNS and BIND,* this book's close cousin.

For BIND configuration or operational problems, search the archives of one of the newsgroups or mailing lists on BIND:

- For BIND 4 or 8, Google's archive of the newsgroup *comp.protocols.dns.bind*, at *http://groups.google.com/groups?as_ugroup=comp.protocols.dns.bind&hl=en*.
- The archive of *bind-users*, the mailing list equivalent of *comp.protocols.dns.bind*, at *http://marc.theaimsgroup.com/?l=bind-users*.
- And for BIND 9, the archive of the *bind9-users* mailing list is located at *http://marc.theaimsgroup.com/?l=bind-users*.

For information on the Domain Name System, you should look for relevant RFCs at *http://www.rfc-editor.org/rfcsearch.html* or you can search Google's archive of the newsgroup *comp.protocols.std.dns*, which is located at *http://groups.google.com/groups?as_ugroup=comp.protocols.dns.std&hl=en*. You might also check the BIND section of the Internet Software Consortium's web site, at *http://www.isc.org/products/bind/*.

Discussion

This list is far from comprehensive; there's lots of information about DNS and BIND available on the Internet. If you don't find what you're looking for at one of the places mentioned here, use a good search engine to track down what you're looking for.

See Also

"Handy Mailing Lists and Usenet Newsgroups" in Chapter 3 of *DNS and BIND*.

1.2 Asking Questions You Can't Find Answers To

Problem

You have a pressing question about DNS or BIND and can't find the answer in this book.

Solution

Check one of the relevant mailing lists or newsgroups:

- The BIND Users mailing list, at *bind-users@isc.org,* discusses the operation and configuration of BIND name servers and resolvers. BIND Users is bidirectionally gatewayed to the Usenet newsgroup *comp.protocols.dns.bind.*
- The BIND 9 Users mailing list, at *bind9-users@isc.org,* discusses the operation and configuration of BIND 9 name servers.

You can also try asking me at Cricket's Corner: *http://www.menandmice.com/9000/9300_DNS_Corner.html.* I can't answer every question, but I answer as many as I can.

Discussion

Before asking a question on either of these mailing lists or the newsgroup, be sure to check their archives. See Recipe 1.1 for their locations. If everyone did this, the volume of messages on the mailing lists would drop precipitously, and newbies would get fewer curt or exasperated answers from cranky old-timers like me. (And we'd all live happily ever after.)

You may want to subscribe to one of the mailing lists or the newsgroup above, rather than just posing your question, getting an answer and disappearing until the next question pops into your head. Subscribing guarantees that you'll see any replies (since some folks won't copy you on responses) and will expose you to a wealth of DNS and BIND knowledge.

To subscribe to BIND Users or BIND 9 Users, send a message with the word "subscribe" in the body to *bind-users-request@isc.org* or *bind9-users-request@isc.org*, as appropriate.

See Also

Recipe 1.1 and "Handy Mailing Lists and Usenet Newsgroups" in Chapter 3 of *DNS and BIND*.

1.3   Getting a List of Top-Level Domains

Problem

You need a list of top-level domains (TLDs), possibly to figure out which one your organization belongs in.

Solution

See *http://www.norid.no/domreg.html* for an alphabetical list of top-level domains. See *http://www.norid.no/domreg-alpha.html* for a list of top-level domains alphabetized by country name (instead of the top-level domain label). Each list includes links to the registration authority for each TLD.

Discussion

The most recent edition of *DNS and BIND,* as of this writing, also contains a list of top-level domains as its Appendix A. However, that list does not include the new generic top-level domains (e.g., *biz* and *info*), as they were introduced after that edition's publication.

See Also

Appendix A of *DNS and BIND*.

1.4   Checking Whether a Domain Name Is Registered

Problem

You want to check whether a particular domain name is already registered, or who has registered that domain name.

Solution

Use the *whois* service offered by the appropriate registration authority, or use a command-line version of *whois* to look up registration information about the domain name you're interested in.

The Internet Assigned Numbers Authority, or IANA, maintains a list of country-code top-level domains (ccTLDs) at *http://www.iana.org/cctld/cctld-whois.htm,* which includes links to the web pages of those ccTLDs registration authorities. Many of these web pages offer online *whois* lookups. The web site *http://www.allwhois.com/* also includes links to many *whois* lookup facilities.

If your host's operating system includes a command-line *whois* client, you can use that to look up to look up registration information about the domain name. Newer *whois* clients automatically determine which *whois* server to query, so you can simply run:

```
$ whois domain-name
```

Older *whois* clients may require you to specify the *whois* server to use. For these, you can try *tld.whois-server.net*. For example:

```
$·whois -h ca.whois-servers.net risq.ca
```

The *whois* output usually contains information about the registrant (the person or organization that registered the domain name). For example:

```
$ whois isc.org
```

produces output that includes:

```
Registrant:
Internet Software Consortium (ISC2-DOM)
    950 Charter Street
    Redwood City, CA 94062
    US
```

```
Domain Name: ISC.ORG

Administrative Contact, Billing Contact:
   Conrad, David Randolph  (DC396)  drc@ISC.ORG
   Internet Software Consortium
   950 Charter Street
   Redwood City, CA 94063
   1-650-779-7061 (FAX) 1-650-779-7055
Technical Contact:
   Vixie, Paul  (PV15)  paul@VIX.COM
   M.I.B.H., LLC
   950 Charter Street
   Redwood City, CA 94063
   +1.650.779.7000 (FAX) +1.650.779.7055

Record last updated on 04-Mar-2002.
Record expires on 05-Apr-2004.
Record created on 04-Apr-1994.
Database last updated on 14-Mar-2002 09:39:00 EST.

Domain servers in listed order:

NS-EXT.VIX.COM              204.152.184.64
NS1.GNAC.COM               209.182.195.77
```

Discussion

If the registration authority for your prospective top-level domain doesn't offer a *whois* server, or you can't find it, you can look up NS records for the domain name you're interested in. For example:

```
$ dig ns domain-name
```

If the domain name has NS records, it's very likely registered. On the other hand, if a domain name lacks NS records, it may still be registered: some TLDs take a day or more to process a new registration and add the corresponding NS records.

See Also

"Using whois" in Chapter 3 of *DNS and BIND*.

1.5   Registering a Domain Name

Problem

You want to register a new domain name.

Solution

First, find out which registrars can register your domain name.* For the generic top-level domains, this is easy: there's a list of registrars accredited by ICANN, the Internet Corporation for Assigned Names and Numbers, at *http://www.icann.org/ registrars/accredited-list.html*. For other domains, start at *http://www.norid.no/ domreg.html*: each entry is a link to the registry for that particular top-level domain. While the registry may not process registration requests, most registries provide links to their registrars on their web sites.

Next, choose a registrar. The registrars for a single top-level domain may offer different prices for registration and various associated services, such as hosting your zone on their name servers. For the gTLDs (*com*, *net*, and *org*), the cost of registration is usually between $15 and $35 annually (the wholesale price—which you can't get, even if you "know someone in the business"—is $6 per year). For other TLDs, the cost varies considerably.

Finally, register your domain name with the registrar. This is almost invariably a web-based process that involves specifying the domain name you want to register: personal information, such as your name, address, phone number and email address, and the domain names of the name servers you'll use (and possibly their IP addresses). Oh, and some means of allowing the registrar to bill you.

Discussion

Choose your registrar wisely, and not solely on the basis of price. Some registrars offer notoriously poor customer service, and transferring to a different registrar is much more difficult than simply making the right decision the first time. Ask for recommendations from friends and colleagues, check newsgroups for sad tales of woe and, hypothetically, laudatory postings. And make sure you can work with the registrar the way you want to: using a web-based interface, if that's what you prefer, or via fax or a toll-free number (that they answer promptly).

See Also

Recipes 1.6 and 1.8, for registering name servers and changing registrars; and "Registering Your Zones" in Chapter 3 of *DNS and BIND*.

---

* Think of a registrar as a domain name retailer. Their wholesalers are registration authorities, or *registries*, the organizations that manage the registration data itself. A single registrar may handle registration in many different top-level domains.

1.6   Registering Name Servers

Problem

You want to register a name server so that you can then register a domain name and have the corresponding subdomain delegated to it.

Solution

Registering name servers isn't normally done separately from registering a domain name; as part of the registration process for a domain name, you specify the domain names (and, sometimes, the IP addresses) of the name servers that will serve the corresponding zone. If the name servers you specify aren't already registered, the process will register them. See Recipe 1.5 for more information on that process.

If you find that you really need to register a name server independently of registering a new domain name, check your registrar's web site to see if they offer such a service. Network Solutions, for example, lets ISPs register name servers that their customers can then delegate to at *https://www.netsol.com/cgi-bin/makechanges/itts/host*.

Discussion

Before you try to register name servers, make sure they aren't already registered. Any name server that has had even one subdomain of a top-level domain delegated to it is registered with that top-level domain's registry.

Also note that you shouldn't register a host that's not a name server, even if your registrar will let you. Some registrars (and their registries) don't check whether the host you're registering actually has any subdomains delegated to it. But if you register, say, your web server, you may have a hard time changing that information on short notice, and you may forget that your registry's name servers are giving out answers about your web server. Then, when you move your web server and change its address in your zone data, you'll wonder why some people are still trying the web server's old address.

See Also

Recipe 1.5 for registering a domain name.

1.7   Registering a Reverse-Mapping Domain

Problem

You want to register the reverse-mapping domain that corresponds to your network.

Solution

Start by determining whether your reverse-mapping domain is already registered and, if not, which of its parent domains is registered. If your network is, say, 192.168.0/24, try looking up an SOA record for *0.168.192.in-addr.arpa*. If you find an SOA record, then your network's reverse-mapping domain has been registered. If your network is part of a larger block of networks that your ISP owns, you may find that your ISP has registered it. Contact your ISP and ask them to change the delegation for that domain to your name servers. If you're not sure which email address to use for your ISP, the SOA record will show you the email address (in the second RDATA field) of a technical contact. You can also use the *whois* service offered by one of the regional address registries to look up contact information for your network, including phone numbers; see this recipe's "Discussion" for details.

If you don't find an SOA record, peel off the domain name's leading label and a dot and try looking up an SOA record for the result; in this example, you'd look up an SOA record for *168.192.in-addr.arpa*. If that turns up an SOA record, use that record's email address or the associated *whois* information (again, see the "Discussion") to find out whom to contact to have your domain delegated. If there's no SOA record, keep peeling off those labels until you find one. If you get all the way to *in-addr.arpa*, you may need to contact your regional address registry to register your network and the corresponding reverse-mapping zone with them.

Discussion

The three regional address registries are APNIC, which serves Asia and the Pacific, ARIN, which handles the Americas, sub-Saharan Africa and the Caribbean, and RIPE, which deals with Europe and Saharan Africa. Each registry runs its own *whois* service, which contains information about all of that registry's registered networks. Here's a list of the registries' *whois* web pages and the domain names of their *whois* servers:

APNIC
> The web page is at *http://www.apnic.net/apnic-bin/whois2.pl*; the *whois* server is at *whois.apnic.net*

ARIN
> The web page at *http://www.arin.net/whois/index.html*; the *whois* server is at *whois.arin.net*

RIPE
> The web page is at *http://www.ripe.net/ripencc/pub-services/db/whois/whois.html*; the *whois* server is at *whois.ripe.net*

Unfortunately, life is a little more complicated for those of us with networks that have network masks whose bit-lengths aren't integer multiples of eight. If you have a network that's smaller than a /24, you'll have to contact your ISP and ask them to follow the instructions in RFC 2317 (described in Recipe 6.3) to delegate control of the reverse-mapping information for your network to you. If you have a network larger than a /24, you'll end up with more than one reverse-mapping domain for your network. For example, if you run 10.0.0/22, you'll need to have all four of the following domains delegated to you:

- *0.0.10.in-addr.arpa*
- *1.0.10.in-addr.arpa*
- *2.0.10.in-addr.arpa*
- *3.0.10.in-addr.arpa*

Woe unto the poor hostmaster who must set up reverse-mapping for a network like 10.0.0/17!

If the length of your network mask isn't evenly divisible by eight and you're trying to determine which of your domain's parents are registered, start by rounding your network's netmask down to the nearest even multiple of eight and looking up an SOA record for the corresponding network. For example, for 10.0.0/22, round down to 10.0/16 and look up an SOA record for *0.10.in-addr.arpa*.

See Also

Recipes 6.2 and 6.3, for delegating subdomains of reverse-mapping domains, and Recipe 6.3, for handling networks smaller than a /24.

1.8 Transferring Your Domain Name to Another Registrar

Problem

You want to transfer your domain name to another registrar, possibly because they're cheaper or because they offer better service, or to consolidate all of your domain names with a single registrar.

Solution

Each registrar has a different transfer process. That process is usually initiated by the registrar you're transferring the domain name *to*, not the registrar you're transferring the domain name *from*. Check your registrar's web site for details.

Nearly all transfer processes will prompt you for the domain name to transfer, information about the administrative contact (and possibly other contacts), and billing information. The registrar you're transferring the domain name to will then send a form to the email address of the administrative contact for the domain name. The administrative contact will probably need to send the form to a particular email address to authorize the transfer and complete the process.

Discussion

Make sure the email address of your domain name's administrative contact is up-to-date before initiating the transfer, or he won't receive the form the transferring registrar sends. (If you're not sure who the administrative contact is, you can use *whois* to find out, as described in Recipe 1.4.) If you need to change the administrative contact, you'll have to do that through your *current* registrar, not the registrar you're transferring to.

See Also

Recipes 1.4 and 1.5, for checking registration and registering a domain.

1.9   Choosing a Version of BIND

Problem

You need to choose which version of BIND to build and install.

Solution

First, decide whether you'll compile your own version of BIND or use a version supplied by your operating system vendor. If you need to run a version of BIND supported by your vendor, that will limit your choices. Often, the version shipped with your operating system isn't very recent. See if your vendor offers a patch that will upgrade that version to something more current—preferably at least BIND 8.2.3.

If you're willing to compile your own version of BIND, all you really need to decide is whether you want to run BIND 8 or BIND 9. For most administrators and most name servers, BIND 9 is a better choice. The latest released version of BIND 9 as of this writing, 9.2.1, supports nearly every feature that the latest version of BIND 8, 8.3.3, supports. Only administrators running extremely busy name servers (those receiving thousands of queries per second) or those that require one of the few features supported only by BIND 8 should consider running it.

Whether you choose to run BIND 8 or BIND 9, use the latest released version. Earlier versions inevitably contain bugs fixed in the newer version, and some contain dangerous vulnerabilities. Check the ISC's BIND Vulnerabilities web page, at *http://www.isc.org/products/BIND/bind-security.html*, to make sure the version you're considering isn't vulnerable.

Discussion

I have sympathy for administrators compelled by corporate policy to run a vendor-supported version of BIND—I come from a big corporate environment myself. Otherwise, I'd issue a blanket recommendation that everyone run the latest released version of BIND. Just be sure you understand what your vendor's support includes. Some vendors limit their support of BIND to fixing bugs in the code. If you're counting on their help with configuration issues, you may be out of luck.

See Also

The ISC's BIND Vulnerabilities web page at *http://www.isc.org/products/BIND/bind-security.html* and "Getting BIND" in Chapter 3 of *DNS and BIND*.

1.10 Finding Out Which Version of BIND You're Running

Problem

You aren't sure which version of BIND you're running, or which version is installed on your host.

Solution

Start the name server and look for version information in its *syslog* output. You don't even need a *named.conf* file for *named* to read:

```
# /usr/sbin/named
Feb 25 17:17:33 bigmo named[54307]: starting BIND 9.2.0
Feb 25 17:17:33 bigmo named[54307]: using 1 CPU
Feb 25 17:17:33 bigmo named[54307]: loading configuration from '/etc/named.conf'
Feb 25 17:17:33 bigmo named[54307]: none:0: open: /etc/named.conf: file not found
Feb 25 17:17:33 bigmo named[54307]: loading configuration: file not found
Feb 25 17:17:33 bigmo named[54307]: exiting (due to fatal error)
```

Even though the name server doesn't start, you can still find the information you need in the output: This name server is running BIND 9.2.0.

Newer BIND name servers will also print their version if you execute them with the *–v* option:

```
$ /usr/sbin/named -v
BIND 9.2.0
```

If you go this route, however, make absolutely sure that the binary you're checking is the one that's running, and that you haven't recently upgraded to a new version of BIND without restarting the daemon.

Discussion

If you don't find the output you're looking for in the *syslog* output, check *syslog.conf* to make sure that you're checking the right file: *named* usually logs to the *syslog* facility *daemon*.

If the name server is already running, you can send it a query for a TXT record attached to the pseudo-domain name *version.bind* in the CHAOSNET class:

```
$ dig version.bind. txt chaos

; <<>> DiG 9.2.0 <<>> version.bind. txt chaos
;; global options:  printcmd
;; Got answer:
;; ->>HEADER<<- opcode: QUERY, status: NOERROR, id: 40457
;; flags: qr aa rd; QUERY: 1, ANSWER: 1, AUTHORITY: 0, ADDITIONAL: 0

;; QUESTION SECTION:
;version.bind.                   CH      TXT

;; ANSWER SECTION:
version.bind.           0       CH      TXT      "9.2.0"

;; Query time: 2 msec
;; SERVER: 192.168.0.1#53(192.168.0.1)
;; WHEN: Mon Feb 25 17:23:53 2002
;; MSG SIZE  rcvd: 48
```

The version appears in after the string "TXT" on the line immediately below the comment ";; ANSWER SECTION:".

Note that it's easy to change the version returned in the TXT record, so if the name server you're checking with *dig* isn't yours, don't take the version as gospel.

See Also

Instructions on changing the version string a name server returns in Recipe 7.1.

1.11   Getting BIND

Problem

You need a copy of BIND to build and install.

Solution

BIND's source code is freely available. The source code for BIND 9.2.1, the latest release of BIND 9 as of this writing, is available via anonymous FTP from *ftp.isc.org* as */isc/bind9/9.2.1/bind-9.2.1.tar.gz*. The source code for the latest BIND 8 release, currently 8.3.3, is available from the same host as */isc/bind/src/cur/bind-8/bind-src.tar.gz*.

Discussion

If you're concerned about support for your operating system, you may want to check your vendor's web site to see if there's a supported patch you can apply to upgrade the version of BIND that came with your operating system to a newer version.

See Also

"Getting BIND" in Chapter 3 of *DNS and BIND*.

1.12 Building and Installing BIND

Problem

You need to build and install BIND.

Solution

Once you've downloaded BIND's source code, building and installing it is usually easy. First, unpack the distribution. The BIND 9 distribution unpacks into its own subdirectory, named for the release, so you can unpack it with:

```
# cd /usr/local/src        or your source directory
# tar -zxvf /tmp/bind-9.2.1.tar.gz
[Lots of output]
# cd bind-9.2.1
```

BIND 8 distributions unpack into the current working directory, so you may want to create a subdirectory for the distribution before unpacking:

```
# cd /usr/local/src
# mkdir bind-8.3.3
# cd bind-8.3.3
# tar -zxvf /tmp/bind-src.tar.gz
[Lots of output]
```

Next, make sure that the build will use the appropriate settings for your operating system. BIND 9 uses the automagical *configure* program to determine what it needs to know about your operating system and the installation environment. You may still want to specify compilation options, alternate installation directories and the like; to find out what aspects of the build and the installation you can configure, read the *README* file in the top-level directory of the distribution, or run *configure --help*. Once you've decided, run *configure* with those options, and once it's finished, run *make*:

```
# ./configure
# make
```

BIND 8 still uses a *Makefile*. To change compilation options, find the subdirectory of *src/port* relevant to your operating system—for example, *src/port/freebsd* for FreeBSD. Edit the *Makefile.set* file in that directory as you see fit, then build BIND with:

```
# make clean
# make depend
# make all
```

Finally, to install either BIND 8 or BIND 9, run:

```
# make install
```

You'll probably need to *su* to root to install the various binaries and libraries.

Discussion

If you have problems building BIND, check the archives of the mailing lists and newsgroups in Recipe 1.1, and any newsgroups specific to your operating system for hints. You might also want to look for BIND in archives of precompiled binaries for your operating system, as described in Recipe 1.13.

See Also

Recipe 1.11 for getting the BIND source code and Recipe 1.13 for getting precompiled copies of BIND, and Appendix C of *DNS and BIND*.

1.13 Getting a Precompiled Version of BIND

Problem

You need a copy of BIND precompiled for your particular operating system.

Solution

Search the software archive for your operating system for a precompiled version of BIND. Here are the locations of precompiled versions of BIND for a few popular operating systems:

FreeBSD 4.6
    BIND 9.2.1: *ftp://ftp.freebsd.org/pub/FreeBSD/ports/i386/packages-5-current/net/bind9-9.2.1.tgz*

Red Hat Linux 7.3
    BIND 9.2.0: *ftp://ftp.redhat.com/pub/redhat/linux/7.3/en/os/i386/RedHat/RPMS/bind-9.2.0-8.i386.rpm*

Solaris 8
> BIND 9.2.1: *http://www.ibiblio.org/pub/solaris/freeware/sparc/8/bind-9.2.1-sol8-sparc-local.gz*

Windows 2000 and XP
> BIND 9.2.1: *ftp://ftp.isc.org/isc/bind/contrib/ntbind-9.2.1/BIND9.2.1.zip*

Discussion

This option doesn't allow any customization of compile-time options, like whether BIND is built multithreaded or with IPv6 support, so I'd recommend compiling your own copy of BIND if you can.

See Also

Recipes 1.11 and 1.12 for getting a copy of BIND and compiling it yourself.

1.14 Creating a named.conf File

Problem

You need to create a *named.conf* file for a name server.

Solution

Use your favorite editor to create the *named.conf* file, usually in the */etc* directory. Nearly every name server's *named.conf* file contains an *options* statement near the beginning specifying the name server's working directory:

```
options {
    directory "/var/named";
};
```

The *options* statement often contains a good deal more than that, too, including access lists, etc.

After the *options* statement, add *zone* statements to configure the name server as authoritative for one or more zones, as described in Recipes 1.15, 1.16, and 1.17. Finally, if you're running a BIND 8 name server, add a special *zone* statement for the root hints file, which tells the name server the domain names and addresses of the root name servers:

```
zone "." {
    type hint;
    file "named.root";
};
```

Check whether your installation came with a root hints file, and make sure the filename in the *file* substatement matches its name. ("*named.root*" is just a common name for the root hints file.) If you don't have a root hints file, see Recipe 2.11 for instructions on downloading one.

Discussion

You must specify—and create!—a working directory for the name server because there's no default. Some operating systems recommend */var/named* or */etc/namedb*, but the choice is really yours: just make sure the directory is on a filesystem that is mounted when the name server starts, and that the directory has enough space for your zone data files.

See Also

Recipes 1.15 and 1.16 for configuring the name server as primary master or slave for a zone, respectively, Recipe 1.17 for configuring the name server as authoritative for more than one zone, and Recipe 2.11 for updating (or downloading) a root hints file.

1.15   Configuring a Name Server as the Primary Master for a Zone

Problem

You want to configure a name server to be the primary master for a zone.

Solution

Add the appropriate *zone* statement to the name server's *named.conf* file.

The *zone* statement specifies the domain name of the zone and the name of the zone data file, and that this name server is the zone's primary master (with type master):

```
zone "foo.example" {
    type master;
    file "db.foo.example";
};
```

Discussion

Make sure you get the punctuation right: BIND name servers are notoriously unforgiving of incorrect syntax. Double-quote the domain name of the zone and the name of the zone data file. Enclose the *type* and *file* substatements in curly braces, and terminate both substatements and the *zone* statement with semicolons.

You must, of course, also create the zone's data file, which contains all of the resource records in the zone, including the zone's SOA record and NS records. That's covered in Recipe 2.1.

Note that this example shows the most basic zone configuration: I didn't use any zone-specific options, such as an access list for transfers of this zone.

See Also

Recipe 2.1, for instruction on creating a zone data file; and "Running a Primary Master Name Server" in Chapter 4 of *DNS and BIND*.

1.16   Configuring a Name Server as a Slave for a Zone

Problem

You want to configure a name server to be a slave for a zone.

Solution

Add the appropriate *zone* statement to the name server's *named.conf* file.

The *zone* statement specifies the domain name of the zone, the IP address of the master name server, the name of the backup zone data file, and that this name server is a slave for the zone (with type slave):

```
zone "foo.example" {
    type slave;
    masters { 192.168.0.1; };
    file "bak.foo.example";
};
```

Discussion

When configuring a slave zone, there's no need to create the backup zone data file: The name server will write the backup zone data file after it has transferred the zone from the master name server you designated. The slave name server will transfer the zone each time its check of its master shows that the master's copy of the zone has a higher serial number than the slave's copy.

The master name server doesn't need to be the zone's primary master. A slave can just as easily transfer a zone from another of the zone's slaves, as long as that slave gets its zone data from the primary master—directly or indirectly. You can even specify that a slave use multiple master name servers: just list their IP addresses in the *masters* substatement in the order in which you want the slave to use them.

It's a good idea to distinguish backup zone data files from zone data files for primary master zones; I use the prefix "bak" instead of "db" for backup zone data files. This cue makes it less likely that I'll try to make changes to a backup (and hence read-only) copy of a zone's data.

Note that this example shows the most basic zone configuration: I didn't use any zone-specific options, such as an access list for transfers of this zone.

See Also

"Running a Slave Name Server" in Chapter 4 of *DNS and BIND*.

1.17 Configuring a Name Server as Authoritative for Multiple Zones

Problem

You want to configure a name server to be authoritative (i.e., primary master or slave) for more than one zone.

Solution

Add multiple *zone* statements to the name server's *named.conf* file. For example, to make the name server the primary master name server for the *foo.example* zone and a slave for the *bar.example* zone, you might use these two *zone* statements:

```
zone "foo.example" {
    type master;
    file "db.foo.example";
};

zone "bar.example" {
    type slave;
    masters { 192.168.0.1; };
    file "bak.bar.example";
};
```

Discussion

A single name server can be authoritative for multiple zones at once. In fact, there are individual name servers on the Internet that are authoritative for over 100,000 zones. Imagine the size of the *named.conf* file on that name server!

The name server's relationship to the zone is defined on a zone-by-zone basis, in the *type* substatement. So a name server can be the primary master for some zones while it's a slave for others. It can't be both primary master and slave for the same zone, however.

The order of the *zone* statements isn't important. They don't depend on each other in any way, so you can list them in any order you like.

See Also

Recipes 1.15 and 1.16 for the syntax of individual *zone* statements, and Chapter 4 of *DNS and BIND*, as usual.

1.18   Starting a Name Server

Problem

You want to start a name server.

Solution

Run the program *named* or, if you're using BIND 8, use *ndc*:

```
# named
```

or:

```
# ndc start
```

Discussion

If root's path doesn't include the directory in which the *named* executable is installed (often */usr/sbin*), you'll have to specify the full path:

```
# /usr/sbin/named
```

The pathname of the file *ndc* executes to start *named* is compiled-in. If it's not correct, you can edit the file *Makefile.set* and set the variable *DESTSBIN* to the directory in which *named* actually lives. Then recompile *ndc* with:

```
# cd bind-distribution-directory/src/bin/ndc
# make clean
# make ndc
```

The *Makefile.set* file you should modify is in the directory *src/port/<os>*, where *<os>* indicates the operating system you run (e.g., *freebsd*).

If you need to start named with command-line arguments, you can specify them on the command-line:

```
# named -c /tmp/named.conf
```

Or, if you use *ndc*, you can specify them after the argument *start*:

```
# ndc start -c /tmp/named.conf
```

See Also

Recipe 3.1 for setting up and using *ndc*.

1.19   Stopping a Name Server

Problem

You want to stop a running name server.

Solution

Use *ndc* (for BIND 8 name servers) or *rndc* (for BIND 9 name servers):

```
# ndc stop
```

or:

```
# rndc stop
```

Discussion

ndc stop and *rndc stop* both tell the running name server to clean up and exit. "Cleaning up," in this age of dynamically updated zones, means writing the zone data files of any "dirty" zones to disk. ("Dirty" zones are zones that have been dynamically updated but not yet written to disk.)

Should you ever need to stop the name server *without* saving "dirty" zones to disk, BIND 9 offers the *halt* command:

```
# rndc halt
```

If you don't have *ndc* or *rndc* at your disposal (and you won't be able to use *rndc* until you've set up *rndc.conf* and a *controls* statement, as described in Recipe 3.2), you can still kill *named* with signals. With BIND 8, use SIGTERM:

```
# kill `cat /var/run/named.pid`
```

With BIND 9, you can use SIGTERM or SIGINT:

```
# kill -INT `cat /var/run/named.pid`
```

See Also

Recipes 3.1 and 3.2 for setting up *ndc* and *rndc*, respectively, and "Controlling the Name Server" in Chapter 7 of *DNS and BIND*.

1.20 Starting named at Boot Time

Problem

You want *named* to start at boot time.

Solution

On many Unixish operating systems, *named* will start automatically if the startup scripts see a *named.conf* file in the right directory, usually */etc*. On others, you just need to make minor changes to a startup configuration file. However, on some Unixish operating systems, you may need to add the necessary lines to the appropriate file or create a special link to start up *named*.

On BSD-based systems, *named* is usually started by one of the startup scripts, such as */etc/rc.network*. Here's the relevant part of */etc/rc.network* in FreeBSD 4.5:

```
case ${named_enable} in
[Yy][Ee][Ss])
    echo -n ' named';        ${named_program:-named} ${named_flags}
    ;;
esac
```

In this case, the variables *named_enable, named_program* and *named_flags* are set in */etc/rc.conf*:

```
named_enable="YES"
named_flags="-t /etc/namedb -u bind"
```

named_program isn't set in */etc/rc.conf*, so it defaults to *named* in */etc/rc.network*.

Note that I use the *−t* and *−u* options to tell *named* to call *chroot()* and to give up root privileges. This requires some special setup; see Recipes 7.7 and 7.8 for details.

If you're running a BSD-based operating system, just edit */etc/rc.conf*, change *named_enable* to "YES" and set the other *named_** variables, if you need to.

On Solaris 8, named is started from */etc/init.d/inetsvc*:

```
SunOS 5.8
#
# If this machine is configured to be an Internet Domain Name System (DNS)
# server, run the name daemon.  Start named prior to: route add net host,
# to avoid dns gethostbyname timout delay for nameserver during boot.
#
if [ -f /usr/sbin/in.named -a -f /etc/named.conf ]; then
        echo 'starting internet domain name server.'
        /usr/sbin/in.named &
fi
```

If you haven't installed the BIND name server as *in.named*, you can adjust the (two!) occurrences of *in.named* in the script appropriately.

If your operating system uses System V Release 4-style startup scripts, *named* is usually started by a shell script called *named* in the */etc/rc.d/init.d* or */etc/init.d* directory. If you create a link in the directory */etc/rc.d/rc3.d* (called something like *S55named*) to */etc/rc.d/init.d/named*, the *rc* script will run the *named* script in *init.d* and start *named* when the system enters run level 3:

```
# cd /etc/rc.d/rc3.d; ln -s ../init.d/named S55named
```

Also, create links called *K55named* in the directories for runlevels 0, 1, and S, also to *../init.d/named*, to kill the *named* process when entering those runlevels.

Discussion

The relevant run level is reflected in the name of the directory the script lives in: On most Unixish operating systems, run level 3 is the default. To execute a script when the system enters run level 5 (the default run level for most Unixes when running X Windows), create a link from the directory *rc5.d*.

The "S" in "S55named" tells *rc* to run the script with the argument *start* when entering the appropriate run level, while the "K" in "K55named" tells *rc* to run it with *kill* as an argument. The "55" tells *rc* when to run the script: after any scripts with lower numbers, before scripts with higher numbers. If your OS starts other servers that depend on name resolution to work, you may need to adjust the "55" to make sure *named* starts before they do. But make sure *named* starts after all of your host's network interfaces are up.

See Also

Recipe 1.18, for starting the name server from the command line.

## CHAPTER 2

Zone Data

2.0 Introduction

With 27 different tiles in an English Scrabble set ("A" through "Z" plus the blanks) and 7 tiles in a rack, you can draw billions of different combinations. And with over 100,000 words in the Official Word List, you can assemble a lot of words from almost any of those combinations.

In DNS, there are fewer than 300 possible types of resource records, and of those, only a handful could be called common. Still, you can do a remarkable variety of interesting things with those records.

All resource records, when written in plain text (as they'd appear in a zone data file), share the following format:

```
[owner] [TTL] [class] <type> <RDATA>
```

The fields in square brackets ("[" and "]") are optional, while the fields between angle brackets ("<" and ">") are mandatory. Recipe 2.1 explains what happens when you leave out one or more of those fields.

The RDATA field often consists of multiple subfields. The number of subfields required depends upon the type of record. For example, SOA records take seven RDATA subfields, while A and NS records need just one.

A zone data file contains the resource records attached to all of the domain names in a zone. A zone's primary master name server loads the zone data file, and the zone's slaves transfer the zone data from the primary master.

2.1 Creating a Zone Data File

Problem

You need to create a data file for a zone.

Solution

Using your favorite editor, create a file in the primary master name server's working directory. Name the file after the zone whose resource records it will contain. For example, for the *foo.example* zone, you might call the zone data file *db.foo.example*.

Begin the file with a *$TTL* control statement.* This tells other name servers (not those authoritative for the zone) how long they may cache records from this zone by specifying the zone's default *time to live*. You can specify the value as an integer number of seconds or as a scaled value: an integer followed by *s* for seconds, *m* for minutes, *h* for hours, *d* for days or *w* for weeks. For example, you can specify a time to live of one day with either:

    $TTL 86400

or:

    $TTL 1d

You can even concatenate two scaled values, like so:

    $TTL 1d12h

Time to live values between one hour and one day are common.

Next, add an SOA record for the zone. The SOA record contains information about the whole zone, including how often the zone's slave name servers should check to see whether the zone has changed. The SOA record begins with the zone's domain name, a specification of the zone's class (which is almost always *IN*, for Internet), and the type mnemonic *SOA*. After the type, the SOA record requires seven fields:

The MNAME field
> Specify the domain name of the zone's primary master name server.

The RNAME field
> Specify an email address at which the administrator of the zone can be reached. Substitute a dot (".") for the "@" in the email address.

The zone's serial number
> If you'll only be changing the zone manually, by editing the zone data file, consider using the format *YYYYMMDDVV*, where *YYYY* is the year, *MM* is the numeric month (from 1 to 12), *DD* is the date, and *VV* is a two-digit version number that starts at 00. This will give you a handy indicator of when you last updated the zone.

The zone's refresh value
> This specifies how frequently slave name servers for the zone should check their master name server to see whether the zone's serial number has been incremented (indicating that the zone has changed). This value isn't particularly important if you use the NOTIFY mechanism, which enables your primary

---

* Assuming you're running a version of BIND newer than 8.2—and you should be.

master name server to *tell* slaves when the zone changes, but values between one hour and three hours are common.

The zone's retry value
> This specifies how often the zone's slave name servers should check their master name server after a check of the serial number has failed. As with refresh, this isn't that important if you use NOTIFY, but values between 15 minutes and 1 hour are common.

The zone's expire value
> This specifies how long the zone's slave name servers will continue responding if they're unable to reach their master name server to find out the current serial number. Since this determines how long your slaves will answer queries for data in the zone in the event of an outage, you should make it fairly long. Values of several weeks to a month are common.

The zone's negative caching time to live value
> This determines how long other name servers can cache negative answers given out by the zone's authoritative name servers. One such negative answer is *NXDOMAIN*, which indicates that the domain name the remote name server looked up doesn't exist in the zone. This value should be fairly low, between 15 minutes and 3 hours.

Here's a sample SOA record for the *foo.example* zone:

```
foo.example.    IN    SOA    ns1.foo.example.    (
                hostmaster.foo.example.
                2002040700
                1h
                15m
                30d
                1h )
```

Since we ran out of room for the record on the first line, we ended the line with "(", which tells the name server to treat all text between the "(" and a successive ")" as though it were on a single line. (We could also have just kept typing the whole record on a single line, but that would have been hard to read.)

Finally, add NS records listing the domain names of the authoritative name servers for the zone. You probably specified these name servers when you registered your domain name.

```
foo.example.    IN    NS    ns1.foo.example.
foo.example.    IN    NS    ns2.foo.example.
foo.example.    IN    NS    ns.isp.net.
```

Discussion

The domain names in the resource records all end in dots to keep the name server from appending the origin to them. The default origin for a zone data file is just the domain name of the zone, which in this case is *foo.example*, so we could have written the SOA record as:

```
@    IN    SOA    ns1    (
     hostmaster
     2002040700
     1h
     15m
     30d
     1h  )
```

("@" is short for "the current origin.")

Since these first several resource records in the zone are all attached to the same domain name (*foo.example*, in our example), you can specify the domain name for just the first of them and begin the rest of the records with whitespace (spaces or tabs):

```
@    IN    SOA    ns1    (
     hostmaster
     2002040700
     1h
     15m
     30d
     1h  )

     IN    NS    ns1.foo.example.
     IN    NS    ns2.foo.example.
     IN    NS    ns.isp.net.
```

The name server interprets records that begin with whitespace as belonging to the most recently specified domain name.

See Also

Recipe 1.14 for creating a *named.conf* file, Recipe 1.15 for configuring a primary master name server, and Chapter 4 of *DNS and BIND*.

2.2   Adding a Host

Problem

You need to add a host to DNS.

Solution

Add an A and a PTR record for the host to the appropriate zones (which are almost certainly two different zones: a forward-mapping and a reverse-mapping zone). For example, to add a host called *host.foo.example* with the IP address 10.0.0.1 to DNS, you could add this record to the *foo.example* zone data file:

```
host.foo.example.    IN    A    10.0.0.1
```

And you'd add this record to the zone data file for the reverse-mapping zone, which might be *10.in-addr.arpa*, *0.10.in-addr.arpa*, or *0.0.10.in-addr.arpa*, depending on how you break up administration of your reverse-mapping domain:

```
1.0.0.10.in-addr.arpa.    IN    PTR    host.foo.example.
```

Discussion

You're free to take advantage of the origin in the file to abbreviate the resource records. For example, if you're adding the A record to a line in the zone data file in which the origin is *foo.example*, you can write:

```
host   IN   A   10.0.0.1
```

If you're adding the PTR record on a line in which the origin is 0.0.10.in-addr.arpa, you can write:

```
10   IN   PTR   host.foo.example.
```

Since the default class is *IN*, for Internet, you can leave out the IN, too.

It's important to add PTR records for your hosts. Without PTR records, your hosts' addresses won't map to domain names, so they won't be able to access services that require reverse mapping, and your network management software may not identify them automatically.

You may also want to add other records for the host. If the host's domain name might appear on the right side of an email address, add an MX record specifying where mail addressed to the host should be delivered.

See Also

Recipe 2.4, for how to add an MX record; Recipe 2.9 to limit how long the records can be cached, Recipe 2.10 to learn how to handle multihomed hosts, and Chapter 4 of *DNS and BIND*.

2.3   Adding an Alias

Problem

You need to create an alias from one domain name to another.

Solution

Add a CNAME record to the zone that the alias belongs in. For example, to make *a. foo.example* an alias for *b.bar.example*, add this CNAME record to the *foo.example* zone data file:

```
a.foo.example.   IN   CNAME   b.bar.example.
```

Discussion

Note that a CNAME record makes the alias equivalent to the target of the alias. Queries for any types of record attached to the alias will end up as queries for the same type of record, but attached to the domain name the alias points to. Consequently, you can't add any other types of records to a domain name that is an alias.

You also shouldn't use aliases on the right side of other types of records, such as NS and MX records. The consumers of NS and MX records—name servers and mail servers, respectively—don't expect aliases on the right side and therefore don't process them correctly. The only kind of record that allows an alias on the right side is the CNAME record itself: You can point an alias to another alias, as long as the alias chain ends at a non-alias domain name. Make sure the chain isn't more than eight links long, though, and beware alias loops.

Finally, note that the CNAME record belongs in the zone that contains the domain name of the alias, not the target of the alias.

See Also

Recipe 2.6 to learn how to set up virtual web hosts; and Chapter 4 and the "Using CNAME Records" section of Chapter 16 in *DNS and BIND*.

2.4   Adding a Mail Destination

Problem

You need to add a mail destination to DNS.

Solution

Add one or more MX records to the zone that contains the domain name of the mail destination. The MX records specify the mail server or servers that accept mail addressed to that mail destination. Each MX record requires a preference value that tells mailers sending mail the order in which to contact the destination's mail servers. The *lower* the preference value, the *more preferred* the mail server.

For example, to tell mailers to send mail addressed to *foo.example* (such as an email message addressed to *hostmaster@foo.example*) to *mail.foo.example*, and *smtp.isp.net* only if *mail.foo.example* isn't up or isn't accepting connections, add these MX records to the *foo.example* zone data file:

```
foo.example.    IN    MX    0 mail.foo.example.
foo.example.    IN    MX    10 smtp.isp.net.
```

Discussion

The preference value is an unsigned, 16-bit number, so between 0 and 65535. The magnitude of the number isn't important: the preference value doesn't represent any particular units. What's important is that the preference values for a domain name's MX records, taken together, tell a sending mailer the order in which it should use the destination's mail servers.

Most mailers will spread the load randomly among mail servers listed at the same preference value. This can come in handy with popular mail destinations: You can list a number of mail servers at the most preferred preference value and sending mailers will distribute the delivery of your mail among those mail servers.

The mail server must be specified as a single domain name, not an IP address. If you use an IP address on the right side of an MX record, mailers—expecting a domain name there—will try to look up the IP address as a domain name. This causes unnecessary queries to the root name servers, and fails to return an IP address, anyway.

It's up to you (or your fellow postmasters) to configure the mail servers to accept mail addressed to the destination. Make sure the most preferred mail exchangers understand that the mail destination is local, and make sure less preferred mail exchangers are configured to relay mail addressed to the destination.

See Also

RFC 2821 for authoritative information on SMTP and use of MX records, and Chapter 5 of *DNS and BIND*.

2.5 Making the Domain Name of Your Zone Point to Your Web Server

Problem

You want the domain name of your zone to point to your web server.

Solution

Add an A record to the domain name of your zone pointing to the IP address of your web server:

```
foo.example.   IN   A   10.0.0.1
```

Discussion

Adding such an A record lets people specify just *http://foo.example/* (leaving out the leading "www") when accessing your web site. Several popular web sites publish their URLs in this form, including CNN.

Many people try to solve this problem by adding a CNAME record to the domain name of the zone, rather than an A record:

```
foo.example.   IN   CNAME   www.foo.example.
```

This, however, is illegal because it violates the dictum that an alias have no records other than a CNAME record associated with it.

If you have multiple web servers, you can add multiple A records for the domain name of your zone:

```
foo.example.   IN   A   10.0.0.1
foo.example.   IN   A   10.0.0.2
foo.example.   IN   A   10.0.0.3
```

The records are given out in round robin order, by default, as described in Recipe 2.7.

See Also

Recipe 2.3 for more information on CNAME records, Recipe 2.6 for pointing a domain name at a particular URL, not just a particular web server, and Recipe 2.7, for a description of round robin.

2.6   Pointing a Domain Name to a Particular URL

Problem

You want people who access one of your domain names to reach a particular URL.

Solution

Add an A record to the zone to which the domain name belongs, pointing to the IP address of the web server:

```
mylink.foo.example.   IN   A   10.0.0.1
```

Then configure the web server to direct browsers requesting *http://mylink.foo.example* to the appropriate directory on your web server.

Discussion

Most of this solution is configured on the web server using a facility called "virtual hosts." The web server needs to associate your domain name, when it appears in the

HTTP/1.1 "Host" header, with a particular "document root," a directory in the web server's document tree.

If the domain name of the web server is in a zone run by someone else, or you already have a domain name in your zone pointing to the address of the web server, you can use a CNAME record instead of an A record:

```
mylink.foo.example.    IN    CNAME    www.isp.net.
```

This way, if the IP address of the web server changes, your domain name will continue to point to the right place.

Of course, if someone else runs the web server, you'll need their cooperation to set up the association between *mylink.foo.example* and the appropriate directory.

See Also

Recipe 2.5 for pointing a domain name at a web server, the Apache Software Foundation's online documents on virtual hosts at *http://httpd.apache.org/docs/vhosts/name-based.html* and *http://httpd.apache.org/docs-2.0/vhosts/*, and "HTTP/1.1 Virtual Hosts" in Chapter 3 of *Apache: The Definitive Guide*.

2.7   Setting Up Round Robin Load Distribution

Problem

You want to set up round robin for a domain name.

Solution

Just add multiple A records to the domain name. For example:

```
www.foo.example.    IN    A    10.0.0.1
www.foo.example.    IN    A    10.0.0.2
www.foo.example.    IN    A    10.0.0.3
```

In successive answers to queries for *www.foo.example*'s address, the *foo.example* name servers will rotate the order in which they return the A records, moving the first A record to the end of the list after each response.

Discussion

All modern name servers give out resource records in round robin order by default. Only very old name servers (before BIND 4.9) don't support round robin.

Remember that round robin isn't load *balancing*. The name server has no idea how busy the web servers that serve *www.foo.example*'s content are, or even whether they're all responding. If the name server at 10.0.0.1 were to crash, the name server would still give out its address first a third of the time. For true load balancing, you need something more than just DNS.

See Also

Recipe 3.18 for details on how round robin works and how to disable it.

2.8 Adding a Domain Name in a Subdomain Without Creating a New Zone

Problem

You want to add a domain name in a subdomain of your zone, but don't want to create a new zone and delegate it from your current zone.

Solution

Just add the records associated with the new domain name, specifying the subdomain in the domain name. For example, to add the domain name *a.b.foo.example* to the *foo.example* zone, you could add this record to the *foo.example* zone data file:

```
a.b.foo.example.   IN   A   10.0.0.4
```

Doing this implicitly creates the subdomain *b.foo.example* and the domain name *a.b.foo.example*. The subdomain *b.foo.example* is part of the *foo.example* zone (as is the domain name *a.b.foo.example*), and will be included in transfers of the zone to slave name servers.

If the origin in the zone data file is *foo.example*, the default, you can also write the record as:

```
a.b      IN   A   10.0.0.4
```

Discussion

Sometimes the solution to a problem is just the most obvious of the possibilities. That's the case both with setting up round robin and with this problem. But many administrators—even the very experienced—aren't accustomed to adding domain names to their zones that have multiple labels to the left of their zones' domain names. They think of the domain names in their zones as always having the format *host.domain-name-of-zone*, rather than any number of labels ending in the domain name of the zone.

See Also

For more on intrazone subdomains, see "Creating a Subdomain in the Parent's Zone" in Chapter 9 of *DNS and BIND*. If you do want to delegate the subdomain and create a new zone, see Recipe 6.1.

2.9 Preventing Remote Name Servers from Caching a Resource Record

Problem

You want to prevent remote name servers from caching one or more records in your zone.

Solution

Give the record (or records) an explicit—and low—time to live (TTL). For example, to keep other name servers from caching your web server's addresses, you could add these A records to the zone data file:

```
www.foo.example.    1    IN    A    10.0.0.1
www.foo.example.    1    IN    A    10.0.0.2
www.foo.example.    1    IN    A    10.0.0.3
```

Specify the explicit TTL between the domain name owner of the record and the class field. By default, the value is an integer number of seconds. You can also use a scaled value, as you would in the *$TTL* control statement.

Discussion

Note that the TTLs for the three *www.foo.example* A records are the same; that's no accident. If you were to use different TTLs for records in the same RRset (of the same type, and attached to the same domain name), a remote name server might age only some of them out, leading to unpredictable results. Consequently, modern name servers notice this misconfiguration and "trim" mismatched TTLs within a single RRset to the smallest TTL of the group.

Why did I use a TTL of one instead of zero? After all, a zero TTL would seem to say, "Don't cache this record." Unfortunately, TTLs of zero tickle a bug in some older name servers, which age out the records before returning them to the resolver that initiated the query. D'oh!

See Also

Recipe 2.1 for the syntax of scaled values, and "Changing TTLs" in Chapter 8 of *DNS and BIND*.

2.10   Adding a Multihomed Host

Problem

You want to add a multihomed host to DNS.

Solution

Add multiple A records to the host's domain name, one per IP address. For example, for a file server with two network interfaces, you might add these records:

```
fs.foo.example.    IN    A    10.0.0.9
fs.foo.example.    IN    A    192.168.0.9
```

To handle reverse mapping for the host, add one PTR record to each of the appropriate two reverse-mapping zones:

```
9.0.0.10.in-addr.arpa.    IN    PTR    fs.foo.example.
```

and

```
9.0.168.192.in-addr.arpa.    IN    PTR    fs.foo.example.
```

Discussion

Clients looking up the address of *fs.foo.example* will see both IP addresses, and can choose which one to use (though most clients will just use the first address returned). Remember that, by default, they'll be returned in round robin order.

For troubleshooting purposes, you may want to add two more A records, each of which maps to just one of your multihomed host's addresses. For example:

```
fs-eth0.foo.example.    IN    A    10.0.0.9
fs-eth1.foo.example.    IN    A    192.168.0.9
```

This lets you test whether a particular network interface on the file server is up, by pinging *fs-eth0.foo.example*, for instance. You probably shouldn't add PTR records mapping the addresses back to these interface-specific names, though: most software can't handle multiple reverse mappings for a single IP address.

See Also

Recipe 2.7 for the behavior of round robin, and Chapter 4 of *DNS and BIND*.

2.11 Updating a Name Server's Root Hints File

Problem

You need to update a name server's root hints file.

Solution

FTP a copy of the most recent root hints file from *ftp.rs.internic.net*. It's called *named.root*, in the directory *domain*.

Discussion

The root hints file, which tells a name server the domain names and addresses of the root name servers, doesn't need to be updated often. The "current" version dates to August 1997, and the file can be slightly out-of-date without causing adverse effects. Still, you should probably check every six months or so to see if it's changed.

If you do download a new root hints file, remember to change the name of the file to whatever you have defined in your *zone* statement for the root hints, and then reload the name server.

See Also

"The Root Hints Data" in Chapter 4 and "Keeping the Root Hints Current" in Chapter 7 of *DNS and BIND*.

2.12 Using a Single Data File for Multiple Zones

Problem

You want to use a single data file for multiple zones.

Solution

Create a "template" zone data file. Make sure that all of the owner names of records in the zone are "@" (short for the origin) or relative; that is, written without a trailing dot. For example:

```
@   IN   SOA   ns1.isp.net. hostmaster.isp.net. (
      2002040900
      3600
      900
      604800
      3600  )
```

```
            IN   NS   ns1.isp.net.
            IN   NS   ns2.isp.net.

            IN   MX   smtp.isp.net.

            IN   A    192.168.0.99

      www IN   CNAME   @
```

Add *zone* statements to your name server's *named.conf* file, configuring it as primary master for the various zones, and specifying the "template" zone data file in the *file* substatement each time. For example:

```
zone "foo.example" {
    type master;
    file "db.template";
};

zone "bar.example" {
    type master;
    file "db.template";
};

zone "baz.example" {
    type master;
    file "db.template";
};
```

Since each *zone* statement sets the default origin to the domain name of the zone in the data file, the SOA record and NS records will always end up attached to the right domain name, and the rest of the records will end up "translated" into the zone.

Discussion

This technique will only work if all of the zones are very similar—nearly identical, in fact. The zones must contain the same number and mix of records, and the records in the zones can only differ by the domain name of the zone. For example, if the domain name *www.foo.example* is an alias for *a.foo.example* in the *foo.example* zone, then *www.bar.example* will be an alias for *a.bar.example* in the *bar.example* zone.

The name server must be the primary master for all of the zones; there's no way to set up an equivalent slave name server that uses the same backup zone data file for all of its zones, since name servers write fully qualified domain names to backup zone data files.

Also, none of the zones can be dynamically updated, since dynamic updates to a zone would cause the name server to rewrite the zone data file, and the rewritten zone data file would also contain fully qualified domain names.

See Also

Recipe 2.1 for understanding the default origin of a zone data file.

2.13 Using Multiple Data Files for a Single Zone

Problem

You want to break a zone into multiple data files, possibly to organize the large number of resource records logically.

Solution

Use the *$INCLUDE* control statement in your top-level zone data file, which interpolates the contents of another file. For example, to include the contents of the file *db.foo.example.hosts* into the data file for the zone *foo.example*, you could use this *$INCLUDE* control statement:

```
$INCLUDE db.foo.example.hosts
```

Discussion

The origin in the included file is, by default, the same as the origin in the file that includes it. If you'd like to change the origin in the included file, specify the new origin as the second argument to the *$INCLUDE* control statement:

```
$INCLUDE db.subdomain.foo.example.hosts subdomain.foo.example
```

On the line after the *$INCLUDE* statement, the origin reverts to its previous setting.

See Also

Recipe 2.8, which explains how to create a subdomain within the same zone.

2.14 Resetting Your Zone's Serial Number

Problem

You need to reset your serial number to some low value, possibly because you inadvertently added a digit to it.

Solution

If you've accidentally incremented your serial number to a value larger than $2^{32} - 1$ (4,294,967,295), first find out what your current serial number is—because it probably isn't what you think it is (the serial number is only 32 bits large). The easiest way to do this is to use a query tool, such as *dig*, to look up your zone's SOA record:

```
$ dig soa foo.example

; <<>> DiG 9.2.1 <<>> soa foo.example
;; global options:  printcmd
;; Got answer:
;; ->>HEADER<<- opcode: QUERY, status: NOERROR, id: 4335
;; flags: qr aa rd ra; QUERY: 1, ANSWER: 1, AUTHORITY: 2, ADDITIONAL: 2

;; QUESTION SECTION:
;foo.example.                     IN      SOA

;; ANSWER SECTION:
foo.example.            86400   IN      SOA     ns1.foo.example. hostmaster.foo.
example. 2002021239 3600 900 2592000 3600
```

If the current serial number is less than 2,147,483,647, add 2,147,483,647 to the serial number. Wait for all of your zone's slave name servers to pick up the new version of the zone (if you're using NOTIFY, that shouldn't take long). Then set the serial number to your target.

If the current serial number is larger than 2,147,483,647, just set the serial number to the number you want.

Discussion

Whahuh? Why on Earth does this work?

Name servers compare serial numbers using *sequence space arithmetic*, which ain't your grandpa's 'rithmetic. In sequence space arithmetic, you have a finite set of integers, but each number has a "next" number. After 0 comes 1, then 2, all the way to 4,294,967,295 ($2^{32} - 1$). The next number after 4,294,967,295 is 0. Think of it like a clock: The hour after 1:00 is 2:00, and the hour after 12:00 is 1:00.

Half of the numbers are larger than any given number, and the other half are smaller. With a set of 2^{32} possible serial numbers, half ($2^{31} - 1$, actually) are larger than any given serial number, and half are smaller.

Consider the serial number 1,000,000,000. The next $2^{31} - 1$ serial numbers, 1,000,000,001 through 3,147,483,647, are larger. The $2^{31} - 1$ serial numbers after that, 3,147,483,648 through 4,294,967,295 ($2^{32} - 1$) and 0 to 999,999,999, are smaller. Yes, Alice, in the world of serial numbers, 3,147,483,648 is *smaller* than 1,000,000,000.

So when you add 2,147,483,647 ($2^{31} - 1$) to a serial number, you're actually adding the largest increment possible—add a larger number and the result will actually be *smaller* than the old serial number, and your zone's slaves won't transfer the zone.

Once all the slaves have the new zone, you can simply set the serial number to the serial number you want, which is now considered larger than the current serial number.

If you're not comfortable with this New Math, try out the script *reset_serial.pl*, included in the *tar* file that accompanies this book (see the Preface for where to get it). *reset_serial.pl* takes as arguments your current serial number and the serial number you want to get to, and tells you how to get there.

There's also a brute force method for resetting your serial number: set the serial number to your target in the zone data file. Then delete your zone's backup data files on all of your slaves and restart *named*. Your slave name servers won't have any choice but to transfer the zone, regardless of its serial number.

This won't work if you don't have administrative control of all of your slaves, of course, and it has all the elegance of using a flat-head screwdriver as a chisel.

See Also

"Starting Over with a New Serial Number" in Chapter 7 of *DNS and BIND*, and RFC 1982 for an explanation of serial number arithmetic.

2.15   Making Manual Changes to a Dynamically Updated Zone

Problem

You want to edit a zone data file by hand, but the zone is dynamically updated.

Solution

On a BIND 8 name server, stop the name server with *ndc stop*, delete the zone's dynamic update log file (whose name is the name of the zone data file with *.log* appended, by default) and the IXFR log file, if any (whose name is the zone data file's plus *.ixfr*). Then edit the zone data file and start the name server.

On a BIND 9 name server, stop the name server with *rndc stop*, delete the zone's journal file (whose name is the zone data file's with *.jnl* on the end), edit the zone data file and start the name server again.

On a BIND 9.3.0 or newer name server, you can freeze the zone with *rndc freeze*, edit the zone data file, and unfreeze the zone with *rndc unfreeze*.

Discussion

With dynamic zones, it's better to make all changes to the zone using dynamic updates. However, sometimes that's just not practical.

The problem is that, with most BIND name servers, if you edit a zone data file while the name server is running, you can lose your changes. When you restart the name server (reloading dynamic zones doesn't work), the name server will rewrite the zone data file if it has received any dynamic updates to the zone that haven't yet been written to the zone data file. What happens to your changes? Poof! They disappear without a trace, like so many dot-coms. You need to stop the name server before editing the zone data file. And that means your name server may miss dynamic updates while you're manually editing the zone data file, so be quick about it!

Also, when you edit the zone data file manually, the changes you make don't get entered into the dynamic update log—the *.log* file, for BIND 8, and the *.jnl* file for BIND 9. When the name server loads the zone data file and then checks the content of the log file, it discovers a gap: It's missing the record of the last change, the one you made manually. So you have to delete the log file before loading.

The price of deleting the log file is that your zone's slaves won't be able to get an incremental zone transfer on their next try, since the record of the last change—necessary to get them up-to-date—is missing. They'll request an incremental zone transfer but receive a full zone transfer instead.

The BIND 9.3.0 name server has two new *rndc* commands, *freeze* and *unfreeze*, which allow you to suspend and resume the processing of dynamic updates to a zone. *freeze* also deletes the log file. So you can *rndc freeze* the zone, edit the zone data file, then *rndc unfreeze*.

See Also

Recipe 5.19, to learn how to use the *nsupdate* program to modify a zone.

2.16   Moving a Host

Problem

You want to move a host from one address to another.

Solution

At least one TTL before the move, reduce the TTL on the host's A record and PTR record to a low number, like 60 seconds. For example, say you're planning on moving the host *z.foo.example*. If its current A record looks like this:

```
z.foo.example.    86400    IN    A    192.168.0.254
```

Reduce the TTL at least a day (86,400 seconds) ahead of time, like this:

```
z.foo.example.    60    IN    A    192.168.0.254
```

At the same time, reduce the TTL on the host's PTR record:

```
254.0.168.192.in-addr.arpa.    60    IN    PTR    z.foo.example.
```

Then, after you've moved the host, change the A record to reflect the host's new address and restore the TTL:

```
z.foo.example.    86400    IN    A    10.0.0.254
```

Delete the old PTR record and add one (to the appropriate zone data file!) for the new address:

```
254.0.0.10.in-addr.arpa.    86400    IN    PTR    z.foo.example.
```

Discussion

You need to reduce the TTL on the old records ahead of time to keep name servers from caching them just before the move. If you left the TTL alone, a remote name server could cache the old address just before you made the change, and it would take some time for that record to time out. If you don't use NOTIFY, you should also add in the refresh time of the zones the records are in, since it could take that long for the lower TTL records to make it out to all of your slaves.

This technique applies to more than just A and PTR records, of course. You could just as easily use it to change MX records or any other record type. If it's a name server you're moving, however, or you need to change your zone's NS records, see Recipes 6.6 and 6.7.

Notice that the new PTR record may well belong in a different zone data file than the old one.

See Also

Recipe 2.9, for an explanation how to reduce the TTL on a single record; Recipes 6.6 and 6.7, for moving a name server and changing all of a zone's name servers; and "Changing TTLs" in Chapter 8 of *DNS and BIND*.

2.17 Mapping Any Domain Name in a Zone to a Single IP Address

Problem

You want to map every domain name in a zone to a single IP address.

Solution

Add an A record to the zone attached to the wildcard domain name. For example:

```
*.foo.example.   IN   A   10.0.0.1
```

Discussion

Technically, this record doesn't map *every* domain name in the zone to 10.0.0.1. In fact, the wildcard domain name doesn't apply to domain names in the zone data file. Say you also had the domain name *ns1.foo.example* in the *foo.example* zone:

```
ns1.foo.example.   IN   A   192.168.0.1
```

The wildcard domain name *wouldn't* match queries for the address of *ns1.foo.example*, which is probably a good thing, since *ns1.foo.example* has a different address. The wildcard domain name wouldn't apply to domain names that own other types of records, either. For example, you might have this record in the zone:

```
text.foo.example.   IN   TXT   "Text comment"
```

Queries for the address of *text.foo.example* would return an empty answer, because *text.foo.example* has no addresses.

So what *does* the wildcard domain name apply to? Queries for domain names in the zone that don't appear in the zone data file, which means any domain name you can think of that ends in *foo.example*, doesn't appear in the *foo.example* zone data file, and isn't part of a delegated subdomain of *foo.example*.

Wildcard domain names can own other types of records, too. Take, for example, this CNAME record:

```
*.foo.example.   IN   CNAME   foo.example.
```

This creates aliases from any domain name in the zone without explicit records attached to the domain name *foo.example*. So iif you leave out explicit records for *www.foo.example*, someone looking up *www.foo.example* would find that domain name is an alias for *foo.example*. Someone looking up *zaphod.beeblebrox.foo.example* would find that it, too, is an alias for *foo.example*—assuming you didn't have any records attached to the domain name *zaphod.beeblebrox.foo.example*, that is. So you might think of a wildcard as a "default" domain name for a zone: any explicit domain name in the zone has only the records you give it, but the wildcard applies to every other domain name in the zone.

As the *zaphod.beeblebrox.foo.example* example suggests, wildcards can match more than one label. In fact, a wildcard matches zero or more labels. The wildcard domain name in the CNAME record wouldn't match just *foo.example*, though, since even at zero labels, *.foo.example* has one more dot than *foo.example*.

See Also

"Wildcards" in Chapter 16 of *DNS and BIND*.

2.18 Adding Similar Records

Problem

You want to add a number of records that differ only slightly.

Solution

Use the *$GENERATE* control statement to specify a template that the name server will use to generate a group of similar records. For example, to add a series of PTR records that differ only by a single digit, you could use this *$GENERATE* control statement:

```
$GENERATE 11-20 $.0.168.192.in-addr.arpa. PTR dhcp-$.foo.example.
```

Your BIND name server will read the range (11–20) and it will also read the template (*$.0.168.192.in-addr.arpa. PTR dhcp-$.foo.example.*) from the *$GENERATE* control statement. Then it will iterate through the range, replacing any dollar signs ("$") in the template with the current value, creating 10 PTR records:

```
11.0.168.192.in-addr.arpa. PTR dhcp-11.foo.example.
12.0.168.192.in-addr.arpa. PTR dhcp-12.foo.example.
13.0.168.192.in-addr.arpa. PTR dhcp-13.foo.example.
...
20.0.168.192.in-addr.arpa. PTR dhcp-20.foo.example.
```

Discussion

$GENERATE supports a limited set of record types: A, AAAA, CNAME, DNAME, NS and PTR. Also, the template can't contain a TTL or a class field, just a type.

If you want to get fancy, you can also step through the range using the range format *start-stop/range*. So *0–100/2* would count from 0 to 100 by twos.

BIND 8.2 introduced *$GENERATE* to the world. BIND 9.1.0 introduced *$GENERATE* to the BIND 9 releases.

Note that, unlike the *$INCLUDE* and *$ORIGIN* control statements, *$GENERATE* is only supported by BIND name servers; you can't use it in a zone data file on a Microsoft DNS Server, for example.

See Also

"Subnetting on a Non-Octet Boundary" in Chapter 9 of *DNS and BIND*, and Section 6.3.6 of the BIND 9 Administrator Reference Manual.

2.19   Making Your Services Easy to Find

Problem

You want to make it easy for users to find the services you offer.

Solution

Give your servers "functional" domain names. For example, most users will expect to find an organization's FTP server at the domain name *ftp.domain-name-of-zone*. In most cases, the domain name can be an alias for the canonical name of the host running the service; that's not possible with name servers or mail servers, though.

Other common functional domain names include:

domain-name-of-zone
> The zone's domain name, by convention, owns one or more A records that point to the organization's web server, and one or more MX records that tell mailers where to deliver mail addressed to the organization's users.

imap.domain-name-of-zone
> An IMAP mail server.

mail.domain-name-of-zone
> An SMTP mail server. Note that this domain name can't be an alias; it must own an A record. Moreover, the mail server must recognize itself as this domain name in order to prevent mail loops.

ns[N].domain-name-of-zone
> The authoritative name servers for your zone. Since there are often more than one, use an integer to distinguish between them: *ns1*, *ns2*, etc. Or, for the unapologetically geeky, *ns0*, *ns1*, etc. Note that these domain names *can't* be aliases; they *must* own A records.

ntp.domain-name-of-zone
> An NTP (Network Time Protocol) server. If you have more than one, disambiguate them by using *ntp1*, *ntp2*, etc.

pop.domain-name-of-zone
> A POP mail server.

smtp.domain-name-of-zone

> An alternative to *mail.domain-name-of-zone*. As with *mail.domain-name-of-zone*, this must own an A record.

www.domain-name-of-zone

> This convention is so common it's almost not worth discussing, but most users expect to find an organization's web site here.

Discussion

One big benefit of using functional domain names is that you can move a service from one host to another by changing only the A or CNAME record for the functional domain name, and without changing the configuration of every client of that service. For example, if you moved your NTP server from *a.foo.example* to *b.foo.example*, you could just change the *ntp.foo.example* CNAME record to:

```
ntp.foo.example.    IN    CNAME    b.foo.example.
```

Assuming you'd configured your NTP clients to refer to your NTP server by the domain name *ntp.foo.example*, you wouldn't have to make any changes to your clients' configuration.

The domain names of mail servers and name servers are special because of the way they're used. The domain name of a name server will usually appear in an NS record, delegating a zone to that name server. A name server sending that NS record in a referral will only add A records for the name server's domain name to the response. If the domain name owns a CNAME record, the name server won't find it.

Likewise, mail servers sending mail to your email addresses expect to find A records for the mail servers you list in your MX records. If you use CNAME records, they won't find the address they're after.

Also, if one of your backup mail servers receives the email, it will "trim" the list of MX records by removing itself and any less-preferred mail servers. If it doesn't recognize itself in the list because you've used an alias in an MX record, it may try to send mail to itself, or to a less-preferred mail server.

2.20   Storing the Location of a Host in DNS

Problem

You want to store the location of a host in your zone data.

Solution

Depending on what you mean by "location," add either a TXT or LOC record to the host's domain name.

Many administrators want to store a descriptive location for the host in DNS. For example, you might want to specify that the host *a.foo.example* is in on your Building 20's level C, near post C3K. To do that, you might add this TXT record to your zone:

```
a.foo.example.    IN    TXT    "Building 20, level C, post C3K"
```

If, on the other hand, you'd like to specify the host's geographical location (i.e., its latitude, longitude, and altitude), you can add a LOC record to your zone. For example, if *a.foo.example* is also at 40 degrees, 2 minutes, 0.373 seconds north latitude; 105 degrees, 17 minutes, 23.528 seconds west longitude; and 1,638 meters altitude, you could add this LOC record to your zone:

```
a.foo.example.    IN    LOC    40 2 0.373 N 105 17 23.528 W 1638m
```

Discussion

The TXT record is enormously versatile, since you can put just about *anything* into the RDATA. Just remember that only people who know to look up the TXT records for a domain name will find the data you store there. Also, if you add multiple TXT records to a domain name, there's no guarantee of the order in which the name server will return them.

The LOC record, on the other hand, is absolutely specialized: it only stores geographical location data. The format is exactly as I've shown it above, with separate RDATA fields for degrees, minutes, and seconds, followed by N for north, S for south, E for east, and W for west. And you can use negative elevation values if you happen to use a colocation facility in Death Valley.

If you're not sure what your hosts' latitude, longitude, and altitude are and you can't persuade your boss that you need a new GPS receiver to find out, you can use Etak's Eagle Geocoder (*www.geocode.com/eagle.html-ssi*) or AirNav's Airport Information, (*www.airnav.com/airports/*) to find the values for your address or a nearby airport, respectively.

See Also

For more information on LOC records, see the "Location" section of Chapter 16 of *DNS and BIND*, RFC 1876, or Christopher Davis's excellent web site at *http://www.ckdhr.com/dns-loc/*.

2.21 Filtering a Host Table into Zone Data Files

Problem

You want to filter an existing host table, such as an */etc/hosts* file, into zone data files.

Solution

Use a tool such as *h2n* to filter your host table into the corresponding zone data files. With *h2n*, you specify the domain name of a forward-mapping zone to create as the argument to the *–d* option and the networks associated with that zone as the argument to one or more *–n* options. For example, the following command would build data files for the *foo.example* and *168.192.in-addr.arpa* zones:

```
% h2n -d foo.example -n 192.168
```

These zone data files would each contain a SOA record and an NS record pointing to the local host, as well as A records or PTR records for hosts in */etc/hosts* on the 192.168/16 network. Additional options allow you to create other records, including NS records pointing to other name servers.

Discussion

You can get a copy of *h2n* from the tar ball that accompanies *DNS and BIND*, located at *ftp.oreilly.com/published/oreilly/nutshell/dnsbind/dns.tar.Z*. Also, Andris Kalnozols of Hewlett-Packard has enhanced *h2n* significantly; he makes his souped-up version available at *ftp.hpl.hp.com/pub/h2n/h2n.tar.gz*.

There are other tools available for filtering host table-format data into zone data files; *h2n* is only one option. Take a look at the contents of *bind-contrib.tar.gz*, available in the same directory as the latest BIND 8 release, for some of your options.

See Also

Recipe 1.11 for how to get a copy of BIND (or *bind-contrib.tar.gz*), and "Tools" in Chapter 4 of *DNS and BIND*.

## CHAPTER 3

BIND Name Server Configuration

3.0   Introduction

The configuration of BIND name servers has grown fiendishly complex since the old BIND 4 name servers. Back then, all you needed was four, maybe five configuration directives. Nowadays, most of the 10 or so configuration statements can have a nested structure with countless substatements—nearly 100 for the *options* statement in the latest BIND 9 name server!

This chapter shows how to put those configuration statements and substatements together in sensible ways to produce useful results, like by differentiating the responses a name server gives out based on the querier's IP address (Recipe 3.17). Related recipes are grouped together, beginning with recipes about configuring a name server's control channel (Recipes 3.1 through 3.3) and progressing into more intricate, more arcane subjects, including dynamic update (Recipes 3.10 and 3.11) and forwarding (Recipes 3.14, 3.15, and 3.16).

When adapting these recipes for use in a name server's *named.conf* file, remember these syntactic rules:

- Terminate each statement and each substatement with a semicolon. It's just like buying toys for your kids: if each one gets an identical semicolon, everybody's happy. If you forget a semicolon for one, or somebody gets a colon or a period instead, there's hell to pay.

- Enclose all lists (of substatements, addresses, whatever) in curly braces, even if the list only contains one element—or, for a *forwarders* substatement, no elements!

- Double-quote all filenames and domain names.

- Define keys and ACLs before you use them.[*]

---

[*] With newer versions of BIND 9, you can refer to keys and ACLs before you define them.

3.1 Configuring a Name Server to Work with ndc

Problem

You want to use *ndc*, the name daemon controller, to control a BIND 8 name server.

Solution

Add a *controls* statement to the name server's *named.conf* file. The *controls* statement tells the name server to create a control channel and to listen on that channel for control messages from *ndc*. BIND 8 supports two kinds of control channels:

unix
> A Unix domain socket that the name server creates on the local filesystem. *ndc* sends messages to the name server by writing to the Unix domain socket.

inet
> A TCP socket that the name server listens on. *ndc* sends messages to the name server by connecting to the TCP socket.

By default, BIND 8 name servers use a *unix* control channel, creating a Unix domain socket with a path compiled into the *named* code. Normally, *ndc* is compiled with the same path.

To specify an alternate pathname, use the *unix* substatement of the *controls* statement:

```
controls {
    unix "/var/run/ndc" owner 0 group 0 perm 0660;
};
```

The first argument to the *unix* substatement is the path to use when creating the Unix domain socket. Successive arguments may appear in any order, and specify the user ID and group ID to use when creating the socket, as well as the permissions to use. (You must use numeric IDs, not user or group names.) Make sure the socket isn't writeable by anyone who shouldn't be able to control the name server.

To tell *ndc* to write to a Unix domain socket other than its default, use the *–l* command-line option, which takes the path to the socket as an option argument. For example:

```
# ndc -l /var/run/ndc
```

To use an *inet* control channel, use the *inet* substatement:

```
controls {
    inet * port 953 allow { localhost; };
};
```

The first argument is the IP address of the network interface the name server should listen on for control messages; "*" means all of them. Successive arguments specify the port to listen on and an access control list that determines who can connect to the port.

To tell *ndc* to connect to a particular address and port, use the *–c* command-line option, which takes an IP address and a port number, separated by a slash, as an option argument. For example:

```
# ndc -c 127.0.0.1/953
```

Discussion

The Solaris operating system doesn't properly check the permissions on Unix domain sockets. Consequently, the name server will create a separate directory for the socket by default, and will set the permissions on that directory to allow access only to authorized users.

BIND 8's *inet* control channels, because they use source IP addresses to identify and authorize control messages, aren't secure. Use *unix* control channels if you can.

BIND 8 doesn't have a default port for control messages, so you must specify one. BIND 9, however, uses port 953 by default, so I usually use port 953 on BIND 8 name servers, too.

unix and *inet* control channels aren't an either-or proposition: You can use both at once if you want to. As I've said, though, *inet* control channels are fairly dangerous.

Note that BIND 9 uses a different program, *rndc*, to control the name server.

See Also

Recipe 3.2 for configuring *rndc*, *ndc*'s BIND 9 counterpart, and "ndc and controls (BIND 8)" in Chapter 7 of *DNS and BIND*.

3.2   Configuring a Name Server to Work with rndc

Problem

You want to use *rndc*, the remote name daemon controller, to control a local BIND 9 name server.

Solution

By far the easiest way to get *rndc* working with a name server is to use *rndc-confgen*, a program shipped with the BIND distribution. *rndc*, unlike *ndc*, its BIND 8 counterpart, requires a configuration file to work properly. The configuration file's syntax, mercifully, is very similar to that of *named.conf*. But rather than learning the new syntax, you can run *rndc-confgen* on the host that will run the name server to generate a useable configuration file. For example, running *rndc-confgen* might produce output like this:

```
$ rndc-confgen
# Start of rndc.conf
key "rndc-key" {
        algorithm hmac-md5;
        secret "LctVnbqQQPHiZJ80ZwnFDA==";
};

options {
        default-key "rndc-key";
        default-server 127.0.0.1;
        default-port 953;
};
# End of rndc.conf

# Use with the following in named.conf, adjusting the allow list as needed:
# key "rndc-key" {
#        algorithm hmac-md5;
#        secret "LctVnbqQQPHiZJ80ZwnFDA==";
# };
#
# controls {
#        inet 127.0.0.1 port 953
#                allow { 127.0.0.1; } keys { "rndc-key"; };
# };
# End of named.conf
```

The beginning of the output (the uncommented part) is the contents of *rndc.conf*, *rndc*'s configuration file. *rndc* will expect to find it in a particular location. If you're not sure what that location is, running an innocuous command like *rndc status* will tell you where it's looking:

```
# rndc status
rndc: neither /etc/rndc.conf nor /etc/rndc.key was found
```

Save the contents of the file there.

The commented part of the file belongs in the name server's *named.conf* file. If you haven't already added a *controls* statement, you can add it to *named.conf* as-is.

Discussion

rndc-confgen appeared in BIND 9.2.0. The configuration files it generates, however, work with older versions of BIND 9, too. So if you're running a version prior to 9.2.0, you can still build 9.2.0 and use the *rndc-confgen* program from that distribution.

With BIND 9.2.0 and later, there's an even easier way to get this working: just run *rndc-confgen –a* on the host that will run the name server. This will write a key definition to the file */etc/rndc.key*, which *rndc* and *named* will then use to negotiate a control channel between them. If you use this option, make sure you don't have a *controls* statement in *named.conf* or an *rndc.conf* file—either of those would override the automatic configuration.

See Also

"rndc and controls" in Chapter 7 of *DNS and BIND*.

3.3   Using rndc with a Remote Name Server

Problem

You want to use *rndc* to manage a remote name server.

Solution

If you used *rndc-confgen* to configure a name server's control channel, the name server's *named.conf* file probably contains *key* and *controls* statements like these:

```
key "rndc-key" {
        algorithm hmac-md5;
        secret "LctVnbqQQPHiZJ8oZwnFDA==";
};

controls {
    inet 127.0.0.1 port 953
    allow { 127.0.0.1; } keys { "rndc-key"; };
};
```

Modify the *controls* statement so that the name server listens on all of the local host's IP addresses for control messages, not just the loopback address. Also, change the access control list in the *allow* substatement to allow connections from the address where you'll run *rndc*. It'll end up looking something like this:

```
controls {
    inet * port 953
    allow { 127.0.0.1; 192.168.0.7; } keys { "rndc-key"; };
};
```

On the host you want to run *rndc* from, create an *rndc.conf* file. (The file normally belongs in the */etc* directory.) Add a *key* statement identical to the one in *named.conf*:

```
key "rndc-key" {
        algorithm hmac-md5;
        secret "LctVnbqQQPHiZJ8oZwnFDA==";
};
```

Then add an *options* statement, specifying the default name server to control and the default key to use to sign commands:

```
options {
    default-server 192.168.0.1;
    default-key "rndc-key";
};
```

rndc should now work from the command line with a single argument. For example:

```
# rndc reload foo.example
```

Discussion

If the name server's *named.conf* file didn't have a *controls* statement to begin with, add one similar to the *controls* statement in the solution. Then add a *key* statement defining a key to use to sign control messages. You can generate a key with the *dnssec-keygen* program that's included with the BIND distribution:

```
$ dnssec-keygen -a HMAC-MD5 -b 128 -n HOST rndc-key
Krndc-key.+157+22603
```

See Recipe 7.9 for instructions on how to drive *dnssec-keygen*.

The file *Krndc-key.+157+22603.key* contains:

```
rndc-key. IN KEY 512 3 157 XvqePraEZOjNklEMu5lfzw==
```

Add a *key* statement to the name server's *named.conf* file defining the new key:

```
key "rndc-key" {
    algorithm hmac-md5;
    secret "XvqePraEZOjNklEMu5lfzw==";
};
```

Add the same *key* statement to the *rndc.conf* file on the host you'll run *rndc* from, as well as an *options* statement like the one shown above.

If you need to control more than one name server from a single host, add *server* statements to *rndc.conf*. The argument to the *server* statement is either the name or the address of the name server. (If you use a name, the name must resolve to the address of the name server.) In each *server* statement, you can define a different key to use to sign control messages to that server. For example:

```
server ns2.foo.example {
    key ns2.foo.example.key;
};
```

Of course, you'll also need *key* statements for each unique key.

Once you've set up *rndc.conf*, you can tell *rndc* to control a particular name server with the *–s* command-line option:

```
# rndc -s ns2.foo.example flush
```

Make sure the argument you specify with *–s* matches the argument you used in the *server* statement *exactly* or *rndc* won't find the corresponding key.

See Also

Recipe 3.2 for setting up *rndc* with a local BIND 9 name server, Recipe 7.9 for instructions on using *dnssec-keygen*, and "rndc and controls (BIND 9)" in Chapter 7 of *DNS and BIND*.

3.4   Allowing "Illegal" Characters in Domain Names

Problem

You need to configure a BIND 8 name server to allow one or more domain names that include illegal characters in your zone.

Solution

Use the *check-names* substatement within the zone's *zone* statement in *named.conf*. For example:

```
zone "foo.example" {
    type master;
    file "db.foo.example";
    check-names warn;
};
```

warn tells the name server to alert you to illegal domain names with messages sent to *syslog*, by default. You can also choose *ignore*, which tells the name server to shut up and say nothing about illegal domain names.

Discussion

The whole notion of "illegal" domain names disappeared in BIND 9, which did away with name checking. You can include underscores, punctuation, and almost anything else in a domain name and load it on a BIND 9 name server. That's not a particularly good idea in most cases, but you can.

Many of you still run BIND 8 name servers, though, and they check domain names. In fact, they won't load primary master zones with illegal domain names in them, by default, so you may need to change these settings.

You can set BIND 8's name-checking behavior for all zones by using *check-names* as an *options* substatement. As an *options* substatement, *check-names* also specifies the context in which an illegal domain name is found:

Primary
> In a zone the name server is the primary master for

Slave
> In a zone the name server is a slave for

Response
> In a response from a remote name server

For example, you could allow illegal domain names in all primary master zones with:

```
options {
        directory "/var/named";
        check-names primary warn;
};
```

It's a bad idea to allow illegal characters in responses from remote name servers, since it could subject your name server and your resolvers to certain attacks.

See Also

"Host Name Checking (BIND 4.9.4 and Later Versions)" in Chapter 4 of *DNS and BIND*.

3.5   Dividing a Large named.conf File into Multiple Files

Problem

You want to divide a name server's *named.conf* file into multiple files.

Solution

Use the *include* statement. For example, to include the file *primary.conf*, which contains all of a name server's primary master *zone* statements, and the file *slave.conf*, which contains the name server's slave *zone* statements, you could add these *include* statements to *named.conf*:

```
include "primary.conf";
include "slave.conf";
```

Discussion

By default, the name server looks for the files you include in its working directory. To include files in other directories, specify the full path to the file. For example:

```
include "/etc/primary.conf";
include "/etc/slave.conf";
```

The *include* statement is usually used as a top-level statement; however, BIND 9.2.0 and later name servers allow *include* within most other statements.

See Also

If a name server is authoritative for so many zones that you need to break up the *named.conf* file, you may also need to use several directories for the zone data files, as described in Recipe 3.6. Also see "Using Several Directories" in Chapter 7 of *DNS and BIND*.

3.6 Organizing Zone Data Files in Different Directories

Problem

You want to organize your zone data files in different directories.

Solution

Specify the full path or a relative path to the zone data files in the zones' *file* substatements. For example:

```
zone "foo.example" {
    type master;
    file "/var/named/masters/db.foo.example";
};

zone "bar.example" {
    type slave;
    masters { 192.168.1.1; };
    file "/var/named/slaves/bak.bar.example";
};
```

Or, using relative paths:

```
zone "foo.example" {
    type master;
    file "masters/db.foo.example";
};
```

```
zone "bar.example" {
    type slave;
    masters { 192.168.1.1; };
    file "slaves/bak.bar.example";
};
```

Relative paths are interpreted relative to the name server's working directory.

Discussion

Splitting zone data files into one directory for primary master zones and one for slave zones is handy, but on a name server with hundreds or thousands of zones, you may still end up with an unwieldy number of zone data files in each directory. On a name server like that, you might create 26 subdirectories, named "a" through "z." Then you could organize data files into subdirectories according to the first letter of the zone's domain name. Or you could create subdirectories after the last label of a zone's domain name, and each of those subdirectories could have subdirectories named for the next-to-last label, and so on, like so:

```
<working directory>
    /example/
    /example/db.foo
    /example/bak.bar
    /arpa/
    /arpa/in-addr/
    /arpa/in-addr/192/
    /arpa/in-addr/192/168/
    /arpa/in-addr/192/168/db.0
```

This makes it easy to find a zone data file and keeps directories small.

See Also

Recipe 3.5 and "Using Several Directories" in Chapter 7 of *DNS and BIND*.

3.7 Configuring a Name Server as Slave for All of Your Zones

Problem

You want to configure a name server as a slave for all of the zones your primary master name server is authoritative for.

Solution

Add *zone* statements of type *slave* to correspond to all of the *zone* statements in your primary master name server's *named.conf* file. You can even use the primary master name server's *named.conf* file as a starting point, changing *master* to *slave* in each *type* substatement and adding *masters* substatements, specifying the master's address. You may also want to change the filename in the *file* substatement.

Discussion

Many new administrators expect BIND to support a single configuration statement that says, "Run as a slave name server for all of the zones this other name server is authoritative for." Unfortunately, no such statement exists; a name server is configured as authoritative for zones on an individual basis.

Converting a primary master's *named.conf* file into a *named.conf* file appropriate for a slave is a piece of cake, though. In fact, I wrote a short Perl script, called *makeslaveconf.pl*, that automates the conversion. It's available in the *tar* file that complements this book; see the Preface for details.

See Also

Recipe 1.16 for instructions on configuring a name server as a slave for a zone.

3.8 Finding an Offsite Slave Name Server for Your Zone

Problem

You need to find an offsite slave name server for one or more of your zones.

Solution

Ask your ISP whether slave name service is included in the package of services they offer you. If not, ask whether they offer the service for an additional cost.

If your ISP is unable or unwilling to handle slave name service for your zones, there are alternatives available. Nominum offers free slave name service for noncommercial use at *http://www.secondary.com/*. Nominum also operates a commercial slave-hosting service, called GNS (Global Name Service), at *http://www.nominum.com/services/gns/*, as does UltraDNS, at *http://www.secondarydns.com/*.

Finally, you may want to consider trading slave name service with another organization, say a partner company or a university you have a close relationship with.

Discussion

Far too many organizations have a single point of failure in their DNS infrastructure: all of their authoritative name servers on the Internet are located on the same subnet, behind a single router. While many of these organizations would *like* to have an external slave name server, they're often scared off by the perceived expense of such a solution. But remember that you probably don't need to set up your very own offsite slave; many companies run slave name servers that are authoritative for thousands of zones, and they'd be willing to load your zone, too, for a reasonable sum of money.

See Also

Recipe 1.16 for instructions on configuring a name server as a slave for a zone.

3.9   Protecting a Slave Name Server from Abuse

Problem

You want to protect a slave name server from abuse by the maintainers of the zone.

Solution

Use the BIND 9 *min-refresh-time*, *min-retry-time*, *max-transfer-time-in*, *max-transfer-idle-in*, and *additional-from-auth* substatements.

min-refresh-time and *min-retry-time* are useful in guarding against the zone's administrator's either accidentally or deliberately setting his zone's refresh or retry times too low. For example:

```
zone "bar.example" {
    type slave;
    masters { 192.168.0.199; };
    file "bak.bar.example";
    min-refresh-time 3600;    // 1 hour minimum refresh
};
```

max-transfer-time-in and *max-transfer-idle-in* allow you to specify how long the name server will wait for a transfer of the zone to complete, and how long it will wait while the transfer is idle (i.e., isn't making progress). For example:

```
options
    directory "/var/named";
    max-transfer-time-in 1800;    // max transfer time 30 minutes
    max-transfer-idle-in 900;     // max transfer idle 15 minutes
};
```

Finally, in order to keep the name server from adding records to the additional data section of responses that come from slave zones, use the *additional-from-auth options* substatement

```
options {
    directory "/var/named";
    additional-from-auth no;
};
```

Discussion

You can use *min-refresh-time* and *min-retry-time* as *options* or *zone* substatements. As a *zone* substatement, the limit applies only to that zone. As an *options* substatement, the limit applies to all zones that don't have an explicit limit.

See Also

Recipe 1.16 for instructions on configuring a name server as a slave for a zone and "Zone Transfers" in Chapter 10 of *DNS and BIND*.

3.10 Allowing Dynamic Updates

Problem

You want to allow dynamic updates to one of your zones.

Solution

Use the *allow-update zone* substatement. For example:

```
zone "foo.example" {
    type master;
    file "db.foo.example";
    allow-update { 192.168.0.4; };
};
```

This allows dynamic updates to the *foo.example* zone from the IP address 192.168.0.4. You can specify multiple addresses, or a whole range of addresses, but that's generally a bad idea: You want to restrict dynamic updates as much as possible, since an updater allowed via *allow-update* can make just about any change to the zone.

In fact, if you run a BIND 9 name server and the software sending dynamic updates supports TSIG-signed updates, you should use the new *update-policy* substatement. *update-policy* lets you determine which domain names and records a particular updater is allowed to update. *update-policy* substatements have the following format:

```
update-policy {
    grant|deny keyname nametype domain-name [type [...]];
    [...]
};
```

The *keyname* field is the name of the TSIG key used to sign the dynamic update. The *nametype* is one of these four values:

name

> Matches when the updated domain name is the same as the name in the *domain-name* field.

subdomain

> Matches when the updated domain name is a subdomain (that is, ends in or is the same as) the name in the *domain-name* field.

wildcard

> Matches when the updated domain name matches the wildcard expression in the *domain-name* field. Only the leftmost label in the expression can be a wildcard character.

self

> Matches when the updated domain name is the same as the name of the TSIG key that signed the update. The contents of the *domain-name* field are ignored, but the field needs to be present.

The type is a record type, such as A, MX, and NS. You can use ANY as shorthand for all record types except NXT. If you omit the field, the default is to allow updates to all types except SOA, NS, SIG, and NXT.

So, for example, in order to restrict dynamic updates to A records for the domain name *www.foo.example* to updates signed with the key *update-key*, you could use this *update-policy* substatement:

```
zone "foo.example" {
    type master;
    file "db.foo.example";
    update-policy {
        grant update-key name www.foo.example A;
    };
};
```

Discussion

allow-update really isn't secure, since it authorizes updates on the basis of the source IP address in the dynamic update message. And dynamic updates are UDP-based, so they're easy to spoof. Unfortunately, there's very little software that supports TSIG-signed dynamic updates—yet.

If you allow dynamic updates to a zone, make sure the MNAME field of the zone's SOA record contains the domain name of the primary master name server; ideally, that's where updaters will send their updates.

The *allow-update* and *update-policy* substatements are only meaningful in *zone* statements of type *master*, since you can only modify data on a zone's primary master name server.

See Also

Recipes 3.19 and 3.20, for information on how to send dynamic updates using *nsupdate*; Recipe 5.22, for sending TSIG-signed updates using *nsupdate*; Recipe 8.9, for a more complex example of *update-policy*; Recipes 9.9 and 9.10, to learn how to send updates programmatically; and "DNS Dynamic Update" in Chapter 10 of *DNS and BIND*.

3.11 Configuring a Name Server to Forward Dynamic Updates

Problem

You want a BIND 9 slave name server to forward any dynamic updates it receives from addresses on the local networks for a zone to its master name server.

Solution

Use the *allow-update-forwarding zone* substatement. For example:

```
zone "foo.example" {
    type slave;
    masters { 192.168.0.1; };
    file "bak.foo.example";
    allow-update-forwarding { localnets; };
};
```

The slave name server forwards any dynamic updates it receives to the *foo.example* zone to its master name server, at 192.168.0.1.

Discussion

For the most part, if you make sure that your zone's SOA record contains the domain name of the primary master name server in the MNAME field, you won't need to worry about update forwarding. Most updaters will automatically find your primary master and send their updates there. But if you use a hidden primary master or have ill-behaved clients, you may need this.

Forwarding updates, however, makes IP address-based authorization using *allow-update* even more dangerous than usual, because forwarded updates have the slave name server's source address. If you use update forwarding, you should use TSIG-signed dynamic updates, too. It doesn't matter if a slave forwards a signed update: it still bears the signature.

See Also

Recipe 3.10 for permitting dynamic updates; Recipes 5.19, 5.20, and 5.22 for sending dynamic updates—particularly TSIG-signed updates—using *nsupdate*; Recipes 9.9 and 9.10 for sending updates programmatically; and "TSIG-Signed Updates" in Chapter 10 of *DNS and BIND*.

3.12   Notifying a Slave Name Server Not in a Zone's NS Records

Problem

You want to notify a slave name server not listed in the NS records for a zone of changes to that zone's serial number.

Solution

Use the *also-notify* substatement as a *zone* substatement, to apply only to changes to that zone:

```
zone "foo.example" {
    type master;
    file "db.foo.example";
    also-notify { 192.168.0.2; };
};
```

Or use it as a substatement to the *options* statement, to apply to all zones for which this name server is authoritative:

```
options {
    directory "/var/named";
    also-notify { 192.168.0.2; };
};
```

Discussion

There are lots of reasons not to list a slave name server in a zone's NS records; you've made it a slave because the resolvers that query it frequently look up records in the zone, but you don't want other name servers querying it, for example. This kind of a slave name server is called a *stealth slave*. See Recipe 7.4 for instructions on configuring a stealth slave.

However, you probably want your stealth slave to be alerted of changes to the zone as quickly as the other slaves for the zone. Since the other authoritative name servers for the zone have no automatic way of discovering your stealth slave, you need to explicitly configure the slave's master name server to send it NOTIFY messages. Remember to configure only your stealth slave's master name server to notify it—it'll ignore NOTIFY messages from other name servers.

Note that *also-notify* isn't supported as an *options* substatement in older versions of BIND 8. Support was introduced in BIND 8.2.2.

See Also

Recipe 7.4 for instructions on configuring a stealth slave name server and "DNS NOTIFY (Zone Change Notification)" in Chapter 10 of *DNS and BIND*.

3.13   Limiting NOTIFY Messages

Problem

You want to limit the NOTIFY messages your zone's name servers send to the bare minimum. Unfortunately, by default, your zone's primary master name server will send NOTIFY messages to all of the zone's slaves, *and the slaves will send NOTIFY messages to each other*. (This behavior is intended to deal with slave name servers that get their zone transfers from other slaves.)

Solution

Turn NOTIFY off on the slave name servers, or configure those slaves that act as master name servers to notify only the slaves that transfer from them.

Turning NOTIFY off is simple. Use the *notify* substatement, either within a *zone* statement (to turn off NOTIFY messages for just that zone):

```
zone "foo.example" {
    type slave;
    masters { 192.168.0.1; };
    file "bak.foo.example";
    notify no;
};
```

Or within the *options* statement, to make *not* sending NOTIFY messages the default for this name server:

```
options {
    directory "/var/named";
    notify no;
};
```

To limit NOTIFY messages to just an explicit list of name servers, use the *notify explicit*
substatement and define the list of name servers in an *also-notify* substatement:

```
zone "foo.example" {
    type slave;
    masters { 192.168.0.1; };
    file "bak.foo.eample";
    notify explicit;
    also-notify { 192.168.0.3; };
};
```

notify explicit is supported in BIND 9.1.0 and later, and BIND 8.3.2 and later.

Of course, *notify explicit* also works as an *options* statement.

Discussion

The authoritative name servers for a zone "discover" which other name servers to
notify from the zone's NS records. Normally, all of the zone's authoritative name
servers are listed in the NS records, including the primary master and all of the
slaves. If the primary master is listed in the MNAME (first RDATA) field of the
zone's SOA record, the slaves won't notify it of changes. They *will* send NOTIFY
messages to each other, though.

Though each NOTIFY message is relatively small, a change to a zone with a lot of
name servers can trigger a blizzard of messages, as each slave name server tells every
other slave that the zone has changed. Slaves ignore NOTIFY messages that don't
come from their master name servers, so most of this traffic is wasted. It reminds me
of sitting in the back of the car with my sister:

Mom: You two be quiet!

Me: Yeah, shut up.

Sis: No, *you* shut up.

Since my sister never listened to me and I never listened to my sister, there wasn't
much point in our telling each other to shut up. My mother, of course, needed to tell
both of us, or else we never would have shut up.

See Also

Recipe 3.12 for the use of *also-notify* and "DNS NOTIFY (Zone Change Notification)" in Chapter 10 of *DNS and BIND*.

3.14 Configuring a Name Server to Forward Queries to Another Name Server

Problem

You want a name server to forward queries it can't answer locally to another name server.

Solution

Use the *forwarders options* substatement to configure a forwarder for the name server. For example:

```
options {
    directory "/var/named";
    forwarders { 192.168.0.1; };
};
```

The name server will forward any query it can't answer locally—that is, from authoritative zone data or from cache—to the forwarder.

Discussion

Since a name server configured to use forwarders relies on them for most name resolution, it's a good idea to list multiple forwarders. The name server will query them in the order you list them until it receives an answer. (BIND 8.2.3 and later name servers will first query the one in the list that's responding most quickly, which is even better.)

The default behavior of a name server configured to use one or more forwarders is to revert to iterative name resolution if the forwarders don't respond in about 60 seconds. To tell the name server to rely solely on the forwarders, and never try iterative name resolution, use the *forward options* substatement, set to *only*:

```
options {
    directory "/var/named";
    forwarders { 192.168.0.1; };
    forward only;
};
```

This "forward only" mode is actually preferable to the default behavior, because the forwarding timeout is so long that most resolvers have already given up on the name server before it even begins iterative name resolution.

See Also

Recipe 3.15 for how to forward only queries for certain domain names, Recipe 3.16 for how to configure a name server *not* to forward queries for certain domain names, and "Forwarding" in Chapter 10 of *DNS and BIND*.

3.15 Configuring a Name Server to Forward Some Queries to Other Name Servers

Problem

You want a name server to forward queries for certain domain names to another name server.

Solution

Use a *zone* statement of type *forward* to tell a BIND 8.2 or later or 9.1.0 or later name server to forward queries for domain names that end in the specified suffix to particular name servers. For example:

```
zone "bar.example" {
    type forward;
    forwarders { 10.0.0.9; };
};
```

This tells the name server to forward queries for domain names that end in *bar.example* to the name server at 10.0.0.9.

Discussion

As with the corresponding *options* substatement, you can list multiple forwarders in the *forwarders* substatement.

An alternative to using a forward zone is to use a stub zone. Stub zones are a little like slave zones, in that the name server periodically checks with its master server to see if the zone's serial number has changed. But instead of transferring the whole zone, it retrieves just the zone's SOA and NS records, plus any necessary glue A records, using discrete queries. That's enough information to tell the name server where to begin iterative name resolution of domain names that end in the domain name of the stub zone. For example, here's a stub zone definition very similar to the forward zone defined earlier:

```
zone "bar.example" {
    type stub;
    masters { 10.0.0.9; };
    file "stub.bar.example";
};
```

Rather than sending a recursive query to the name server at 10.0.0.9 for information about any domain name that ends with *bar.example*, this name server would learn the *bar.example* NS records, and send one of those name servers a nonrecursive query for the domain name it needed. It would then follow any successive referrals to find the answer. This is less work for the name server at 10.0.0.9, but it also requires connectivity to any name server the local name server might be referred to.

See Also

Contrast this with Recipe 3.14, which tells you how to configure a name server to forward all queries it can't answer locally, and Recipe 3.16, which explains how to configure a name server *not* to forward certain queries. See "Forward Zones" in Chapter 10 of *DNS and BIND* for more information.

3.16 Configuring a Name Server Not to Forward Certain Queries

Problem

You want to configure a name server not to forward queries for certain domain names.

Solution

Use a null (empty) *forwarders* substatement to override forwarding for queries that would otherwise be forwarded. For example:

```
options {
    directory "/var/named":
    forwarders { 192.168.0.1; };
};

zone "foo.example" {
    type master;
    file "db.foo.example";
    forwarders {};
};
```

Note the empty list of forwarders.

A null *forwarders* substatement will work in master, slave, and stub zones.

Discussion

For primary master and slave zones, such as the primary master zone in the example above, it may not be obvious which queries the name server would forward. It's *authoritative* for *foo.example*, after all, so why would it ever forward a query for a domain name in the zone?

The answer is that the null forwarders list applies not just to domain names in the zone, but to any domain names that end in the domain name of the zone. So in this example, the name server wouldn't forward queries for domain names that ended in *foo.example*, even if those domain names were in delegated subdomains of *foo.example*.

If you need to override forwarding for some domain names but don't want to make the name server authoritative for the zone that has that domain name, use a stub zone, as described in Recipe 3.15. The name server will just get the zone's SOA and NS records, and via discrete queries, not a zone transfer.

There's no way to disable forwarding without at least configuring a stub zone, though. For example, you can't do this:

```
zone "foo.example" {
    type forward;
    forwarders {};
};
```

While this might turn off forwarding for domain names that end in *foo.example*, the name server won't know how to resolve those domain names without at least the *foo.example* NS records.

See Also

Recipes 3.14 and 3.15, and "Forward Zones" in Chapter 10 of *DNS and BIND*.

3.17 Returning Different Answers to Different Queriers

Problem

You want to configure a name server to return different answers to the same query depending on the IP address from which the query is sent.

Solution

Use BIND 9's *view* mechanism to create multiple versions of the zone that will contain the answer, and use the *match-clients* substatement to place the addresses of the queriers in the appropriate view.

For example, to have *www.foo.example* map to the address 192.168.0.10 for internal queries, and to the address 206.168.119.176 for queries from the Internet, create a *db.foo.example.internal* zone data file that includes this A record:

```
www.foo.example.    IN    A    192.168.0.10
```

Then create a *db.foo.example.external* zone data file that includes this record:

```
www.foo.example.   IN   A   206.168.119.176
```

Define an access control list in *named.conf* to match internal IP addresses:

```
acl internal { 192.168/16; };
```

Then configure the two versions of the zone in two *view* statements:

```
view internal {

    match-clients { internal; };

    zone "foo.example" {
        type master;
        file "db.foo.example.internal";
    };

};

view external {

    match-clients { any; };

    zone "foo.example" {
        type master;
        file "db.foo.example.external";
    };

};
```

Discussion

The first *match-clients* substatement that matches a querier's address determines which view the querier sees, so queries from addresses that don't match the *internal* ACL fall through to the external view and are answered from that version of *foo.example*.

The *match-clients* substatement defaults to *any*, so you can leave the substatement out of the external view entirely. However, subtlety is not always a virtue when writing *named.conf* files, so you might want to use an explicit substatement, as I did here, to make the configuration that much easier to grok.

See Also

If you want the name server to return the same answer, but with the records in a different order, see Recipe 3.18. If you need to set up a slave name server for zones in multiple views on your primary master—and you have my sympathy—brace yourself, then read Recipe 3.19. For more information on views, see "Views" in Chapter 10 of *DNS and BIND*.

3.18 Determining the Order in Which a Name Server Returns Answers

Problem

You want a name server to return certain answers in a particular order.

Solution

Use the *rrset-order options* substatement in BIND 8 or BIND 9.3.0 and later.

In BIND 8, *rrset-order* lets you choose to give out answers that include multiple resource records in one of three orders:

cyclic
> The default, often referred to as round robin. The order in which records are returned is rotated between responses, with the first record given out in the previous answer moved to the end in the next answer.

fixed
> Records are always returned in the same order.

random
> Records are returned in a random order.

rrset-order also lets you select the particular answers an order applies to using three qualifiers:

name
> The order only applies to answers to queries for the specified domain name, which may include a wildcard as its leftmost label. The default is "*".

class
> The order only applies to answers to queries in the specified class, which defaults to IN.

type
> The order only applies to queries for the specified type of record. The default is ANY, or any type of record.

The default behavior, then, is equivalent to:

```
options
    rrset-order {
        name "*" class IN type ANY order cyclic;
    };
};
```

So, to return the A records of your web server in a fixed order, you might use:

```
options {
    rrset-order {
        name "www.foo.example" type A order fixed;
    };
};
```

You'd want to make sure that *www.foo.example*'s A records appeared in the correct order in the *foo.example* zone data file, of course.

Versions of BIND from 9.3.0 on support just the *cyclic* and *random* orders.

Discussion

BIND 9 doesn't support *true* round robin, in which the name server tracks the order in which it gives out the records in an answer. Instead, it randomly chooses a starting point in the list of records and then places the remaining records into the response as though the first record had rotated to the beginning. For example, say *www.foo.example* had the following three A records:

```
www.foo.example.    IN    A    10.0.0.1
                    IN    A    10.0.0.2
                    IN    A    10.0.0.3
```

A BIND 9 name server might choose the third A record as the starting point, and then would insert the next two A records (10.0.0.3 and 10.0.0.1) to produce a response in the following order:

```
www.foo.example.    IN    A    10.0.0.3
                    IN    A    10.0.0.1
                    IN    A    10.0.0.2
```

If what you want to do is sort addresses on certain networks to the front of responses, you need to configure the *sortlist*. See Recipe 3.28.

See Also

Recipe 2.7 for setting up round robin and "The rrset-order Substatement" in Chapter 10 of *DNS and BIND* for more information on *rrset-order*.

3.19   Setting Up a Slave Name Server for a Zone in Multiple Views

Problem

You want to configure a BIND 9 name server as a slave for a zone that exists in multiple views on the master name server.

Solution

Configure the slave name server to initiate the transfers of the zone from different source IP addresses, one for each of the views of the zone. Then configure the master name server to make a different view of the zone visible to each of the slave's source addresses.

For example, say the master name server loads two views of the zone *foo.example*:

```
options {
    directory "/var/named";
};

acl internal { 192.168/16; };

view internal {

    match-clients { internal; };

    zone "foo.example" {
        type master;
        file "internal/db.foo.example";
    };

};

view external {

    match-clients { any; };    // match all other IP addresses

    zone "foo.example" {
        type master;
        file "external/db.foo.example";
    };

};
```

If the slave name server has the IP address 192.168.1.1, it would normally only see— and only be able to transfer—the internal version of *foo.example*.

If you add an IP address alias (say, 192.168.1.2) to the slave's network interface, though, you can reconfigure the master to place that one IP address in the external view. Here's how the configuration of the slave might look:

```
options {
    directory "/var/named";
};

acl internal { 192.168/16; };

view internal {

    match-clients { internal; };
```

```
    zone "foo.example" {
        type slave;
        masters { 192.168.0.1; };
        file "internal/bak.foo.example";
        transfer-source 192.168.1.1;
    };

};

view external {

    match-clients { any; };

    zone "foo.example" {
        type slave;
        masters { 192.168.0.1; };
        file "external/bak.foo.example";
        transfer-source 192.168.1.2;
    };

};
```

Here's how the primary master's *named.conf* file might look, after changing the configuration to place the slave's new address in the external view:

```
options {
    directory "/var/named";
};

acl internal { ! 192.168.1.2; 192.168/16; };

view internal {

    match-clients { internal; };

    zone "foo.example" {
        type master;
        file "internal/db.foo.example";
    };

};

view external {

    match-clients { any; };    // match all other IP addresses

    zone "foo.example" {
        type master;
        file "external/db.foo.example";
    };

};
```

There are still minor problems with this configuration as written—NOTIFY doesn't work. When the primary master name server sends NOTIFY messages to the slave, the slave interprets those NOTIFY messages according to the view the source address of the message is in. Since the primary master's address is in the slave's internal view, the slave assumes all NOTIFY messages refer to the internal copy of *foo.example*. Also, the primary will look up the addresses of the slave to send it NOTIFY messages. If the primary's address is in its own internal view, it'll only find the slave's internal address.

To solve this, the master needs two addresses, too: one from which it can look up the slave's internal address and send NOTIFY messages about the internal view, and one from which it can look up the slave's external address and send NOTIFY messages about the external view. And, of course, both the primary master and the slave need to consider the primary's extra address part of its external view. So the primary master's configuration ends up looking like this:

```
// Primary master; has IP addresses 192.168.0.1 and 192.168.0.2

options {
    directory "/var/named";
};

acl internal { !192.168.0.2; ! 192.168.1.2; 192.168/16; };

view internal {

    match-clients { internal; };

    query-source address 192.168.0.1;    // so it sees slave's internal addr

    zone "foo.example" {
        type master;
        file "internal/db.foo.example";
        notify-source 192.168.0.1;        // so the NOTIFY falls into the
                                          // slave's internal view
    };

};

view external {

    match-clients { any; };              // match all other IP addresses

    query-source address 192.168.0.2;    // so it sees slave's external addr

    zone "foo.example" {
        type master;
        file "external/db.foo.example";
        notify-source 192.168.0.2;        // so the NOTIFY falls into the
                                          // slave's external view
    };

};
```

And the slave's configuration looks like this:

```
// Slave; has IP addresses 192.168.1.1 and 192.168.1.2

options {
    directory "/var/named";
};

acl internal { !192.168.0.2; !192.168.1.2; 192.168/16; };

view internal {

    match-clients { internal; };

    query-source address 192.168.1.1;    // so it sees internal addrs

    zone "foo.example" {
        type slave;
        masters { 192.168.0.1; };
        file "internal/bak.foo.example";
        transfer-source 192.168.1.1;    // so it gets the internal view
    };

};

view external {

    match-clients { any; };

    query-source address 192.168.1.2;    // so it sees external addrs

    zone "foo.example" {
        type slave;
        masters { 192.168.0.1; };
        file "external/bak.foo.example";
        transfer-source 192.168.1.2;    // so it gets the external view
    };

};
```

Discussion

Notice that the negation of the new IP address of the slave name server in the definition of the *internal* access control list causes queries from that address—including
zone transfer requests—to fall through to the external view.

See Also

Recipe 3.17 for setting up multiple views on a primary master name server.

3.20 Disabling Caching

Problem

You want to disable caching on a name server.

Solution

Use the *recursion options* substatement:

```
options {
    directory "/var/named";
    recursion no;
};
```

Discussion

Disabling recursion is one of the most effective ways to limit the amount of memory a name server uses. Processing a recursive query often requires a name server to query another name server, and the name server then caches the response. It's caching that causes a name server's memory usage to increase over time; without caching, a name server tends to use the same amount of memory. If a name server treats all queries as nonrecursive, it won't query other name servers and hence won't cache.

Unfortunately, you can't disable recursion on just any old name server. Many name servers serve one or more authorized resolvers, and those resolvers need their recursive queries answered, well, recursively. Name servers used as forwarders must process recursive queries, too. If you want to limit memory utilization on a name server that needs to process recursive queries, see Recipe 3.21.

See Also

Recipe 3.21, for information on limiting how much memory a name server uses, and "A Nonrecursive Name Server" in Chapter 10 of *DNS and BIND*.

3.21 Limiting the Memory a Name Server Uses

Problem

You want to limit the amount of memory a name server uses.

Solution

Use the *max-cache-size options* substatement:

```
options {
    directory "/var/named";
    max-cache-size 10m;       // maximum cache size of 10MB
};
```

This tells the name server to remove old, cached records early (i.e., before they're stale) if the size of the cache reaches the limit. If you set this, you may also want to reduce the cleaning interval (the period at which the name server checks for stale records):

```
options {
    directory "/var/named";
    max-cache-size 10m;       // maximum cache size of 10MB
    cleaning-interval 15;     // clean cache every 15 minutes
};
```

You may also find the *max-cache-ttl* and *max-ncache-ttl options* substatements handy. These limit the time-to-live values of cached records and cached negative responses, respectively. For example:

```
options {
    directory "/var/named";
    max-cache-size 10m;       // maximum cache size of 10MB
    cleaning-interval 15;     // clean cache every 15 minutes
    max-cache-ttl 60;         // limit cached record to a 60s TTL
    max-ncache-ttl 60;        // limit cache neg. resp. to a 60s TTL
};
```

Discussion

The minimum maximum cache size (that is, the smallest you can set the limit) is two megabytes.

max-cache-size isn't supported until BIND 9.2.0, while *max-cache-ttl* is supported as far back as 9.0.0. *max-ncache-ttl*, believe it or not, is supported in BIND 8.2 and later. (It was introduced when BIND name servers began caching negative responses according to the enclosing zone's SOA record, as a safeguard against unintentionally long TTLs.)

Whatever you do, don't set *max-cache-ttl* to zero. If you do, the name server will let useful records expire (the NS records it receives in referrals, say) before it uses them, and you'll see SERVFAIL responses for domain names in zones outside the name server's authority.

Some administrators are tempted to use the *datasize options* substatement to limit the size of the data segment the *named* process uses. Unfortunately, when *named* reaches the *datasize* limit, it exits. And then, of course, you have no name server running at all—though I guess that minimizes its memory utilization.

See Also

Recipe 3.20 and "System Tuning" in Chapter 10 of *DNS and BIND*.

3.22 Configuring IXFR

Problem

You want to configure a slave (and its master) name server to use incremental zone transfers (IXFRs).

Solution

On a BIND 9 name server, you don't need any special configuration: BIND 9 slave name servers request IXFRs by default, and BIND 9 masters automatically create and maintain the journal files they need to respond to IXFR requests.

On BIND 8, however, you need to tell slave name servers to request an IXFR from a particular master in a *server* statement:

```
server 192.168.0.1 {
    support-ixfr yes;
};
```

You also need to configure the master to track changes to zones so it can respond to IXFR requests:

```
options {
    directory "/var/named";
    maintain-ixfr-base yes;
};
```

Discussion

Remember that IXFR only works with dynamically updated zones: the only changes that are logged in the master's journal are those made using dynamic updates. If you manually edit a zone data file, the changes won't make it into the journal. Moreover, a BIND 9 name server won't load a zone that's been edited by hand because it doesn't have the record of the latest change.

See Also

Recipe 3.23 to limit the size of the BIND 8 IXFR log file, Recipe 2.15 for instructions on making manual changes to a dynamically updated zone, and "Incremental Zone Transfer (IXFR)" in Chapter 10 of *DNS and BIND*.

3.23 Limiting the Size of the IXFR Log File

Problem

You want to limit the size of the incremental zone transfer (IXFR) log file.

Solution

Use the BIND 8 *max-ixfr-log-size options* substatement. For example, to limit the size of the IXFR log file to 100K, you'd use:

```
options {
    directory "/var/named";
    maintain-ixfr-base yes;
    max-ixfr-log-size 100k;
};
```

Discussion

Without a configured maximum size for the IXFR log file, a BIND 8 name server will trim the log once it exceeds 50% of the size of the corresponding zone data file. If your chosen maximum is higher than 50% of the size of the zone data file, your maximum will supersede the built-in limit.

Though it's documented earlier, *max-ixfr-log-size* doesn't work until BIND 8.2.1.

You won't need to do this at all with a BIND 9 name server. (In fact, BIND 9 name servers don't understand *max-ixfr-log-size*, so there's no point in trying.) A BIND 9 name server will automatically trim its journal file. Like the sticker says, "No user serviceable parts inside."

See Also

Recipe 3.22 for configuring IXFR on BIND 8 name servers and "Incremental Zone Transfer (IXFR)" in Chapter 10 of *DNS and BIND*.

3.24 Configuring a Name Server to Listen Only on Certain Network Interfaces

Problem

You want to configure a name server so that it listens only on some of the host's network interfaces.

Solution

Use the *listen-on options* substatement:

```
options {
    directory "/var/named";
    listen-on { 192.168.0.1; };
};
```

The name server will only listen on network interfaces that match the address match list. You can specify several addresses; for example, you probably want the name server to listen on the loopback interface:

```
options {
    directory "/var/named";
    listen-on { 192.168.0.1; 127.0.0.1; };
};
```

Discussion

The *listen-on* substatement can come in handy if you're running a name server on a host with lots of IP address aliases. You probably aren't going to configure resolvers to query all of those addresses, or delegate zones to all of them. Just pick one and tell the name server to listen only on that address.

You can also tell the name server not to listen on a particular interface by using an address match list with a negated element:

```
options {
    directory "/var/named";
    listen-on { ! 192.168.0.254; };
};
```

See Also

Recipe 7.2, to learn how to configure a name server to send queries from a particular IP address, and "Configuring the IPv4 Transport" in Chapter 10 of *DNS and BIND*.

3.25 Running a Name Server on an Alternate Port

Problem

You want to run a name server on a port other than 53.

Solution

Use the *listen-on options* substatement. For example:

```
options {
    directory "/var/named";
    listen-on port 1053 { any; };
};
```

If this is a master name server for one or more zones, you can specify the port on which the master is running in your slaves' *masters* substatements. A *zone* statement on the slave might look like this:

```
zone "foo.example" {
    type slave;
    masters port 1053 { 192.168.0.1; };
    file "bak.foo.example";
};
```

Discussion

This configuration requires some explaining. What's the use of running a name server on an alternate port?

The most common reason is to test a name server's configuration. You can configure a name server to listen on a high-numbered port, even start it without root privilege, and use *dig*'s *–p* option (to specify the port number) or *nslookup*'s *set port* command (same thing) to make sure it responds the way you expect.

You might also be running firewall software that does port translation, so that you can translate incoming queries sent to port 53 to whichever port you choose. Or you might just want to run several *named* processes on the same host, acting as master name servers for different versions of the same zone. Of course, you can also use BIND 9's views feature for that, with less overhead.

Specified before the list of master name servers, the port applies to all masters. Sometimes that isn't what you want, because not all of your masters run on an alternate port. If that's the case, BIND 9 name servers support an alternate form:

```
zone "foo.example" {
    type slave;
    masters { 192.168.0.1 port 1053; 192.168.1.1; };
    file "bak.foo.example";
};
```

See Also

"Configuring the IPv4 Transport" in Chapter 10 of *DNS and BIND*.

3.26 Setting Up a Root Name Server

Problem

You want to set up your own root name server.

Solution

Create a data file for the root zone. The data file needs an SOA record for the root zone and NS records for all of your root name servers. For example:

```
$TTL 86400
.    IN    SOA    ns1.corp.example. hostmaster.corp.example.    (
     2002042600 1h 15m 30d 1h )
     IN    NS    ns1.corp.example.
     IN    NS    ns2.corp.example.
```

You'll probably also need to add delegation to the zones at the "top" of your namespace. For example, if most of your internal domain names end in *corp.example*, you'd add NS records delegating *corp.example* to the right name servers:

```
corp.example.    IN    NS    ns3.corp.example.
corp.example.    IN    NS    ns4.corp.example.
```

All of these name servers will require glue A records, too:

```
ns1.corp.example.    IN    A    10.0.0.1
ns2.corp.example.    IN    A    10.1.0.1
ns3.corp.example.    IN    A    10.2.0.1
ns4.corp.example.    IN    A    10.3.0.1
```

Don't forget to delegate the reverse-mapping zones that correspond to your networks:

```
10.in-addr.arpa.    IN    NS    ns3.corp.example.
10.in-addr.arpa.    IN    NS    ns4.corp.example.
```

Then add a new *zone* statement to the name server's *named.conf* file to tell it to load the root zone's data file:

```
zone "." {
    type master;
    file "db.root";
};
```

You can create slave root name servers, too, by adding a *zone* statement like this to their *named.conf* files:

```
zone "." {
    type slave;
    masters { 10.0.0.1; };
    file "bak.root";
};
```

Finally, you should replace the root hints file on your non-root name servers with one that lists your new, internal roots:

```
.     IN   NS   ns1.corp.example.
      IN   NS   ns2.corp.example.

ns1.corp.example.   IN   A   10.0.0.1
ns2.corp.example.   IN   A   10.1.0.1
```

Discussion

Moving to a DNS architecture that uses internal root name servers is a big decision, with implications far beyond what I can cover here. For example, with an internal root architecture, you can't resolve Internet domain names. Make sure you know what you're doing.

See Also

"DNS and Internet Firewalls" in Chapter 11 of *DNS and BIND*.

3.27 Returning a Default Record

Problem

You want a name server to return the same record regardless of the domain name looked up.

Solution

Occasionally, administrators want to set up a name server that maps every domain name to the same IP address. To do that, configure the name server as a root name server, add an A record to the wildcard domain name in the root zone and omit any delegation. For example, the root zone might look like this:

```
$TTL 86400
.     IN   SOA   default-ns.corp.example. hostmaster.corp.example.   (
      2002042600 1h 15m 30d 1h )
      IN   NS   default-ns.corp.example.

default-ns.corp.example.   IN   A   10.0.0.1

*.    IN   A   10.0.0.10
```

Discussion

Most administrators probably take one look at this configuration and think, "Why in the world would I ever need a name server like *that*?" But for some applications, this kind of name server can come in handy. Think of those in-room, high-speed Internet access services that hotels offer: after you connect and get an IP address via DHCP, you reach the service's web site regardless of the URL you type in. This kind of name server could make up part of that solution.

One minor thing to note: BIND 8 and BIND 9 name servers treat wildcard domain names differently. On a BIND 9 name server, the wildcard in the zone above would match all domain names except *default-ns.corp.example* and domain names that end in that string. On a BIND 8 name server, the wildcard *wouldn't* match domain names that end in *example*. You'd need to add another A record to a different wildcard domain name to match those domain names:

```
*.example.    IN    A    10.0.0.10
```

See Also

Recipe 3.26 for instructions on setting up a root name server, and "Internal Roots" in Chapter 11 and "Wildcards" in Chapter 16 of *DNS and BIND*.

3.28   Configuring DNS to Let Clients Find the Closest Server

Problem

You want to set up DNS so that your clients (e.g., FTP NFS or NTP clients) can find the server closest to them.

Solution

If you don't have many servers, and it's relatively easy to determine which server is closest to a client given that client's address, use the *sortlist options* substatement. This allows you to configure a *sortlist*: a set of rules that determine, based on the address from which a query is received, which A records to return first in the response to that query.

Say, for example, that you have three networks: 192.168.0/24, 192.168.1/24, and 192.168.2/24. For clients on 192.168.0/24, servers on 192.168.0/24 are—fairly obviously—closest. The next closest servers are those on 192.168.1/24. For clients on 192.168.1/24, again, servers on the same network, 192.168.1/24, are closest, followed by servers on 192.168.0/24. Finally, for clients on 192.168.2/24, servers on the same network are closest, but servers on 192.168.0/24 and 192.168.1/24 are equally close.

A *sortlist* substatement that would return the A record of the closest server first would look like this:

```
options {
    directory "/var/named";
    sortlist {
        { 192.168.0/24; { 192.168.0/24; 192.168.1/24; 192.168.2/24; }; };
        { 192.168.1/24; { 192.168.1/24; 192.168.0/24; 192.168.2/24; }; };
        { 192.168.2/24; { 192.168.2/24; { 192.168.0/24; 192.168.1/24; };  }; };
    };
};
```

Though this seems hairy, it's not quite as awful as it looks. The *sortlist* is an address match list—just a complicated one. Each term in this sortlist is a pair of address match lists. The first element (192.168.0/24 in the first pair) matches the addresses of some queriers. The name server sorts A records in response to those queriers so that the records appear in the order specified in the second element. For the first pair, that's:

```
{ 192.168.0/24; 192.168.1/24; 192.168.2/24; };
```

Or, A records on 192.168.0/24 first, followed by A records on 192.168.1/24, followed by A records on 192.168.2/24, followed by all other A records. If two networks are equally preferred, they're nested further, as in the last pair.

If you have roughly as many servers as you have zones, and each zone has a preferred server, you can take advantage of your resolvers' search lists to let clients find the closest server. For example, say you'd like your NTP clients to find their closest NTP server automatically. You can create an alias, *ntp.<domain name of zone>*, that always points to the domain name of the closest NTP server for that zone. For example:

```
ntp.denver.corp.example.    IN    CNAME    tick.boulder.corp.example.
```

Then configure the NTP clients on the Denver site (which are presumably in the *denver.corp.example* zone) to use the NTP server named just *ntp*. As long as the search list on the hosts the NTP clients run on begins with *denver.corp.example*, they'll use *ntp.denver.corp.example* as their NTP server.

Discussion

The *sortlist* substatement is supported in all versions of BIND from 8.2 on, and in BIND 9 from BIND 9.1.0 on.

Sortlists can also have a simpler form, too, with single terms rather than pairs. For example:

```
options {
    directory "/var/named";
    sortlist {
        { 192.168.0/24; };
```

```
                  { 192.168.1/24; };
                  { 192.168.2/24; };
          };
    };
```

In this form, the name server will sort answers to queries received from 192.168.0/
24, for example, so that A records on 192.168.0/24 are first, and similarly for the
other two networks.

You can mix the two forms if you like, but be careful, because it's easy to leave out a
curly brace ("{" or "}") .

See Also

Recipe 2.3 for how to create an alias, and Recipes 9.2 and 9.3 for how to configure a
resolver's search list.

3.29   Handling Dialup Connections

Problem

You're running an authoritative name server behind a dial-on-demand connection.

Solution

Designate the name server's zones as dialup zones using the dialup *substatement*:

```
options {
    directory "/var/named";
    dialup yes;
};
```

This tells the name server to concentrate zone maintenance activity into a short
period, and to perform that maintenance once each heartbeat interval. The default
heartbeat interval is one hour. For a slave zone, the name server will refresh once, at
most, during each heartbeat interval, even if the zone's refresh interval is shorter. For
a master zone, the name server will send NOTIFY messages to all slaves when the
zone changes, triggering a dialup and a successive zone transfer.

Discussion

To adjust the heartbeat interval, use the *heartbeat-interval options* substatement. For
example:

```
options {
    directory "/var/named";
    heartbeat-interval 180;     // 3 hours
};
```

You can also use *dialup* as a *zone* substatement, in which case it suppresses zone maintenance traffic for just that zone. This may be useful on a name server that has dedicated connectivity to the Internet, but has a slave or master at the far end of a dialup connection.

See Also

"Running Authoritative Name Servers over Dial-on-Demand" in Chapter 16 of *DNS and BIND*.

## CHAPTER 4

Electronic Mail

4.0 Introduction

Remember when you were little, and it was a thrill to get mail, any mail at all? Post-cards from relatives on vacation, greeting cards, the odd misdirected credit card offer—it didn't matter. I'll bet that if you think back far enough, you can remember a time when it was exciting to get Internet email, too.

Now, of course, most Internet email is spam, but we can dream of a simpler time, before the Nigerian email scam and ordering Viagra on the Internet.

One of the linchpins of getting all of that email into your inbox is DNS. Mail transport agents all over the Internet look up MX records attached to your domain names to determine where to deliver your mail. I showed you the basic syntax of the MX record back in Recipe 2.4, but you also can craft those MX records to designate backup mail servers (Recipe 4.1), multiple, equivalent mail servers (Recipe 4.2), and more. This chapter will show you how.

4.1 Configuring a Backup Mail Server in DNS

Problem

You want to configure a backup mail server for a mail destination.

Solution

Add an MX record for the mail destination, listing the domain name of the backup mail server at a higher preference value (and therefore lower preference) than the main mail server. For example, say the MX record for the mail destination *foo.example*, currently looks like this:

```
foo.example.    IN    MX    10 mail.foo.example.
```

To add *smtp.isp.net* as a backup mail server for *foo.example*, add another MX record to *foo.example* pointing to that mail server, with a preference value higher than 10. For example:

```
foo.example.    IN   MX   20 smtp.isp.net.
```

Discussion

By default, most modern mail software won't accept mail addressed to just any old domain name. You may need to configure the backup mail server to accept mail addressed to the mail destination. But don't configure the mail destination as local to the mail server; the backup mail server should accept the mail but queue it for later delivery to your main mail server.

See Also

Recipe 2.4 for instructions on setting up a mail destination and "MX Records" in Chapter 5 of *DNS and BIND*.

4.2   Configuring Multiple Mail Servers in DNS

Problem

You want to configure DNS so that mail addressed to a destination will be sent to one of a number of equivalent mail servers.

Solution

Add MX records for the domain name of the mail destination, pointing to the domain names of the mail servers, all at the same—and lowest—preference value. For example:

```
foo.example.    IN   MX   10 smtp1.foo.example.
foo.example.    IN   MX   10 smtp2.foo.example.
foo.example.    IN   MX   10 smtp3.foo.example.
```

Discussion

Most modern mail servers that have mail to send to a destination will choose randomly among mail servers with the same preference value. All of these mail servers are the "final destination" for the mail, as far as DNS is concerned, so all should be configured to see the mail destination as local.

If one of the mail servers fails, a mail server trying to send mail to the destination will simply try another of the mail servers.

Using multiple "main" mail servers doesn't preclude your listing one or more backup mail servers, too. Just add MX records pointing to the destination's backup mail servers, with higher preference values than the value you used for the main mail servers. For example:

```
foo.example.    IN    MX    10 smtp1.foo.example.
foo.example.    IN    MX    10 smtp2.foo.example.
foo.example.    IN    MX    10 smtp3.foo.example.
foo.example.    IN    MX    20 backup.isp.net.
```

Mail servers sending mail to the destination will only try the backup mail server if they fail to deliver the mail to all more-preferred mail servers.

See Also

Recipe 2.4 for instructions on setting up a mail destination and Recipe 4.1 for designating backup mail servers for a destination, as well as "MX Records" in Chapter 5 of *DNS and BIND*.

4.3   Configuring Mail to Go to One Server and the Web to Another

Problem

You want mail addressed to a particular domain name to be routed to one mail server, while users specifying that domain name in a URL reach a web server on a different host.

Solution

Since mail servers sending mail to a particular domain name mail destination preferentially use MX records for that domain name, add an MX record to that domain name pointing to the mail server. Web browsers, on the other hand, only look up A records, so attach an A record to the domain name pointing to the address of the web server. For example:

```
foo.example.    IN    MX    10 mail.foo.example.
foo.example.    IN    A     192.168.0.100
```

Discussion

This is less a recipe than a reminder that a single domain name can serve multiple purposes: it can represent a mail destination when it appears on the right side of an email address. It can represent a web site when it appears in a URL. Since some of these services look up different types of records, you simply attach multiple record types to a single domain name to accommodate them.

See Also

Recipes 2.4 and 2.5.

4.4 Configuring DNS for "Virtual" Email Addresses

Problem

You want to add a new "virtual" mail destination to DNS.

Solution

Add an MX record to the appropriate zone with the domain name of the mail destination as the owner name and the domain name of the mail server for that destination on the right side. For example, to route mail addressed to *user@bar.example* to *mail.foo.example*, you could add this MX record to the *bar.example* zone:

```
bar.example.    IN    MX    10 mail.foo.example.
```

Discussion

There's really nothing virtual about the mail destination *bar.example* from a DNS perspective—hence the quotation marks. *bar.example* is a legitimate domain name in a real zone that happens to own an MX record, so it's usable as a mail destination.

Note that the MX record must be added to the correct zone. If you want to direct mail addressed to *bar.example* to a particular mail server, you must add the MX record to the *bar.example* zone data file. It won't do anyone any good in the *foo.example* zone data file: it'll be ignored as out-of-zone data.

mail.foo.example will probably need to be configured to understand that *bar.example* is a local mail destination. Then it's up to the mail server on *mail.foo.example* to decide what to do with mail addressed to individual users at *bar.example*. This might be handled by an aliases file or a virtual user table.

See Also

Recipe 2.4.

4.5 Configuring DNS So a Mail Server and the Email It Sends Pass Anti-Spam Tests

Problem

You want to make sure a mail server and the email it sends pass all DNS-related anti-spam tests.

Solution

First, make sure that any domain names used in return addresses resolve to an MX record or an A record. For example, if the mail server sends out all mail addressed from *user@foo.example*, make sure *foo.example* owns at least an MX record:

```
foo.example.    IN    MX    10 mail.foo.example.
```

Next, make sure that the IP address that the mail server sends mail from reverse-maps to a domain name (that is, that the domain name in *in-addr.arpa* that corresponds to the address has a PTR record attached):

```
2.0.168.192.in-addr.arpa.    IN    PTR    mail.foo.example.
```

Check that the domain name that the mail server's address maps to in turn maps back to that address (that is, the domain name has an A record with the same address on the right side):

```
mail.foo.example.    IN    A    192.168.0.2
```

Finally, check that the domain name your mail software uses in the HELO or EHLO (extended HELLO) SMTP commands is either the same as the domain name you just checked (*mail.foo.example*), or else passes the same forward- and reverse-mapping checks. For example, if your mail server announces itself as *smtp.foo.example*, make sure *smtp.foo.example* maps to an address, and that address maps back to *smtp.foo.example*.

Discussion

Not all mail software performs all of these checks when receiving email, but ensuring that a mail server passes them will help guarantee that the mail it sends won't be refused as spam by the stricter mail servers on the Internet.

See Also

Len Conrad's article "How to Keep Your DNS from Blocking Mail Delivery from your and your Clients' Mail Servers" on his "BIND 8 for NT" web site, at *http://bind8nt.meiway.com/itsaDNSmess.cfm*.

CHAPTER 5

BIND Name Server Operations

5.0   Introduction

Creating zone data and configuring a name server is only the beginning. Managing a name server over time requires an understanding of how to control it and which commands it supports. It takes familiarity with other tools from the BIND distribution, including *nsupdate*, used to send dynamic updates to a name server.

This chapter includes lots of recipes that involve *ndc* and *rndc*, programs that send control messages to BIND 8 and 9 name servers, respectively. These programs let an administrator reload modified zones, refresh slave zones, flush the cache, and much more. The list of commands the name server supports seems to grow with each successive release of BIND, so I've provided a peek at a few new commands in BIND 9.3.0 for the curious.

Several recipes describe how to drive the *nsupdate* program to send dynamic updates. In the brave new world of dynamic zones, an administrator may have to make most of the changes to zone data using dynamic update, rather than by manually editing zone data files. The recipes cover sending plain vanilla dynamic updates (Recipe 5.19), setting prerequisites in a dynamic update (Recipe 5.21), and sending TSIG-signed dynamic updates (Recipe 5.22).

Finally, the chapter covers a few common administrative processes, such as setting up and failing over to a backup master name server, migrating from one domain name to another, and measuring a name server's performance.

5.1   Figuring Out How Much Memory a Name Server Will Need

Problem

You need to figure out how much memory a name server will require.

Solution

While this answer may seem like a cop-out, the only sure-fire way to determine how much memory a name server will need is to configure it, start it, and then monitor it using a tool like *top*. After a week or so, the size of the *named* process should stabilize, and you'll know how much memory it needs.

Discussion

The reason it's so difficult to calculate how much memory a name server requires is that there are so many variables involved. The size of the *named* executable varies on different operating systems and hardware architectures. Zones have a unique mix of records. Zone data files may use lots of shortcuts (e.g., leaving out the origin, or even using a *$GENERATE* control statement) or none at all. The resolvers that use the name server may send a huge volume of queries, causing the name server's cache to swell, or may send just sporadic queries.

See Also

The BIND 9 ARM, section 2.3.

5.2   Testing a Name Server's Configuration

Problem

You want to test a name server's configuration before putting it into production.

Solution

Use the *named-checkconf* and *named-checkzone* programs to check the *named.conf* file and zone data files, respectively. *named-checkconf* reads */etc/named.conf* by default, so if you haven't moved the *configuration* file into */etc* yet, specify the pathname to the configuration file you want to test as the argument:

```
$ named-checkconf ~/test/named.conf
```

named-checkconf uses the routines in BIND (BIND 9.1.0 and later, to be exact) to make sure the *named.conf* file is syntactically correct. If there are any syntactic or semantic errors in *named.conf*, *named-checkconf* will print an error. For example:

```
$ named-checkconf /tmp/named.conf
/tmp/named.conf:3: missing ';' before '}'
```

named-checkzone uses BIND's own routines to check the syntax of a zone data file. To run it, specify the domain name of the zone and the name of the zone data file as arguments:

```
$ named-checkzone foo.example db.foo.example
```

If the zone contains any errors, *named-checkzone* prints an error. If the zone would load without errors, *named-checkzone* prints a message like this:

```
zone foo.example/IN: loaded serial 2002022400
OK
```

Once you've checked the configuration file and zone data, configure the name server to listen on a nonstandard port with the *listen-on options* substatement, and not to use a control channel:

```
controls { };

options {
    directory "/var/named";
    listen-on port 1053 { any; };
};
```

That way, the test name server won't interfere with any production name server you might already have running. Check the name server's *syslog* output (which should be clean, if you ran *named-checkconf* and *named-checkzone*) and query the name server with *dig* or another query tool, specifying the alternate port:

```
$ dig -p 1053 soa foo.example.
```

Once you're satisfied with the name server's responses to a few queries, you can remove the *listen-on* substatement, add a real *controls* statement and put it into production.

Discussion

Even though *named-checkconf* and *named-checkzone* first shipped with BIND 9.1.0, BIND 8's configuration syntax is similar enough to BIND 9's that you can easily use *named-checkconf* with a BIND 8 *named.conf* file. The zone data file format is exactly the same between versions, so you can use *named-checkzone*, too.

See Also

Recipe 3.25, for more information on running a name server on an alternate port.

5.3   Viewing a Name Server's Cache

Problem

You want to view a name server's cached data.

Solution

Use *rndc dumpdb* (BIND 9) or *ndc dumpdb* (BIND 8) to dump the cache to disk, then look through the dump file.

Discussion

BIND 9 name servers only dump the contents of the cache to disk by default, but BIND 8 name servers dump both the contents of cache and authoritative zone data to disk, so you'll have to find the cached records in the file.

To determine which records in a BIND 8 database dump were cached, look at the TTLs and the contents of the comment field. Authoritative zone data will have the nice, round TTLs you configured, while cached records will have had their TTLs decremented by the number of seconds they've been in the cache. Cached records will also have "Cr=" as a comment at the end of the record, giving the credibility level of the record (an indication of the quality of the cached record). For example, these records were cached from an authoritative response from the name server at 128.9.0.107:

```
.       518380  IN      NS      I.ROOT-SERVERS.NET.     ;Cr=auth [128.9.0.107]
        518380  IN      NS      E.ROOT-SERVERS.NET.     ;Cr=auth [128.9.0.107]
        518380  IN      NS      D.ROOT-SERVERS.NET.     ;Cr=auth [128.9.0.107]
        518380  IN      NS      A.ROOT-SERVERS.NET.     ;Cr=auth [128.9.0.107]
        518380  IN      NS      H.ROOT-SERVERS.NET.     ;Cr=auth [128.9.0.107]
        518380  IN      NS      C.ROOT-SERVERS.NET.     ;Cr=auth [128.9.0.107]
        518380  IN      NS      G.ROOT-SERVERS.NET.     ;Cr=auth [128.9.0.107]
        518380  IN      NS      F.ROOT-SERVERS.NET.     ;Cr=auth [128.9.0.107]
        518380  IN      NS      B.ROOT-SERVERS.NET.     ;Cr=auth [128.9.0.107]
        518380  IN      NS      J.ROOT-SERVERS.NET.     ;Cr=auth [128.9.0.107]
        518380  IN      NS      K.ROOT-SERVERS.NET.     ;Cr=auth [128.9.0.107]
        518380  IN      NS      L.ROOT-SERVERS.NET.     ;Cr=auth [128.9.0.107]
        518380  IN      NS      M.ROOT-SERVERS.NET.     ;Cr=auth [128.9.0.107]
```

Remember that dumping the cache to disk has no effect on the contents of the cache. If you want to flush (clear) the cache, see Recipe 5.4.

See Also

Recipe 5.4 and "Controlling the Name Server" in Chapter 7 of *DNS and BIND*.

5.4   Flushing (Clearing) a Name Server's Cache

Problem

You want to flush bad records from a name server's cache.

Solution

If you run a BIND 9.2.0 or newer name server, you can flush the cache with *rndc flush*. With older name servers, you need to kill the name server and restart it to flush the cache. You can do that in one fell swoop with *rndc restart* or *rndc exec*.

Discussion

Clearing the cache is really a side effect of killing the name server, since BIND name servers only store cached data in memory. Since restarting the name server takes time, especially if the name server is authoritative for many zones, *rndc flush* is a better option.

If you run multiple views on your BIND 9.2.0 or newer name server, you can flush the cache in only one view using *rndc flush viewname*. For example:

```
# rndc flush internal
```

BIND 9.3.0 will support flushing all of the records attached to a particular domain name with *rndc flushname*. For example:

```
# rndc flushname cnn.com
```

See Also

Recipe 5.9 for restarting a name server with the same command-line options.

5.5 Modifying Zone Data Without Restarting the Name Server

Problem

You want to modify your zone data without restarting the name server.

Solution

Make the change to the zone data file. For BIND 9, run:

```
# rndc reload domain-name-of-zone
```

For BIND 8, run:

```
# ndc reload domain-name-of-zone
```

If you've modified multiple zones, just list them after *reload*. For example:

```
# rndc reload foo.example bar.example
```

Discussion

Remember to increment the serial number in your zone's SOA record after changing the zone data. The primary master reloads the zone regardless of whether you've incremented the serial number, since the file's modification time has changed, but your zone's slaves only have the serial number to tell them whether the zone has been updated.

Reloading individual zones, as shown above, was introduced in BIND 8.2.1 and again in 9.1.0. With older versions of BIND, just use *rndc reload* or *ndc reload*, as appropriate. That takes a little more time, since the name server checks all zone data files to see which have changed.

If you're reloading a zone that exists in multiple views on a BIND 9 name server, specify the view with *rndc reload domain-name-of-zone class view*. For example:

```
# rndc reload foo.example in external
```

Unfortunately, you can't leave out the class, even though you're unlikely ever to reload a non-Internet class zone.

Telling a BIND 9 name server to reload a dynamically updated zone has no effect, since the name server doesn't expect you to update the zone manually. Telling a BIND 8 name server to reload a dynamically updated zone may work—or you may lose your manual changes. See Recipe 2.15 for instructions on how to make manual changes to a dynamically updated zone.

Dynamic update is, of course, another way to update zone data without restarting the name server; see Recipe 5.19 for details.

See Also

Recipe 2.15, for making manual changes to a dynamically updated zone; Recipe 5.7, for manually initiating a zone transfer on a slave; Recipe 5.19 for modifying a zone using dynamic update; and "Controlling the Name Server" in Chapter 7 of *DNS and BIND*.

5.6 Adding or Removing Zones Without Restarting or Reloading the Name Server

Problem

You want to add a new zone or delete an existing zone without restarting or reloading a name server.

Solution

Add a new *zone* statement to *named.conf* or delete an existing one, then run *rndc reconfig* (for BIND 9) or *ndc reconfig* (for BIND 8).

Discussion

It's nice to avoid restarting a busy name server, since restarting clears the cache and takes time on a name server that is authoritative for many zones. A reload, while it doesn't clear the cache, can take time as the name server checks all of its zone data files to see if they've changed. Using *reconfig* avoids these issues, just scanning *named.conf* for added or deleted zones.

ndc supports *reconfig* as of BIND 8.2.2. At BIND 8.2.3, though, you can also use *ndc reconfig –noexpired*, which prevents the name server from trying to load expired zones.

See Also

"Controlling the Name Server" in Chapter 7 of *DNS and BIND*.

5.7 Initiating a Zone Transfer

Problem

You want a slave name server to initiate a zone transfer immediately.

Solution

Use the command *rndc refresh domain-name-of-zone* (for BIND 9) or *ndc reload domain-name-of-zone* (for BIND 8). For example:

```
# rndc refresh bar.example
```

Discussion

Note that neither command will cause a zone transfer if the master name server has an equal or lower serial number for the zone: the slave will check the serial number, see that its copy of the zone is current and go back to waiting for the next NOTIFY message or for the refresh timer to pop. If you really need to force a zone transfer to a slave, you'll have to delete the backup zone data file and restart—not reload—the name server.

Refreshing or reloading individual zones, as shown above, was introduced in BIND 8.2.1 and again in 9.1.0. With older versions of BIND, just use *rndc refresh* or *ndc reload*, as appropriate. A full reload takes some time on a name server authoritative for lots of zones, since the name server checks all zone data files to see which have changed.

If you're refreshing a zone that exists in multiple views on a BIND 9 name server, specify the view with *rndc refresh domain-name-of-zone class view*. For example:

```
# rndc refresh bar.example in external
```

Unfortunately, you can't leave out the class, even though your slave name server probably doesn't serve any non-Internet class zones.

See Also

"Controlling the Name Server" in Chapter 7 of *DNS and BIND*.

5.8 Restarting a Name Server Automatically If It Dies

Problem

You want a name server to restart automatically if it dies.

Solution

Use the *nanny.pl* Perl script included in the BIND 9 distribution. After you've unpacked the BIND 9 distribution, you'll find *nanny.pl* in *contrib/nanny/nanny.pl*.

nanny.pl runs as a daemon, so just modify the variables at the top of the script as needed and then start it. You may also want to configure your host to start *nanny.pl* at boot time.

There are four variables you may need to customize:

```
$pid_file_location = '/var/run/named.pid';
$nameserver_location = 'localhost';
$dig_program = 'dig';
$named_program = 'named';
```

For example, if you're starting *named* with one or more command-line options, change *$named_program* accordingly, like so:

```
$named_program = 'named -t /etc/namedb -u bind';
```

Discussion

nanny.pl checks every 30 seconds to see if the *named* process exists using *kill −0* against its process ID, and by querying the local name server with *dig*. If either test fails, the script restarts the name server.

There's nothing specific to BIND 9 in *nanny.pl*, so you can use it with BIND 8 name servers, too.

See Also

Recipe 1.18, for starting the name server from the command line.

5.9 Restarting a Name Server with the Same Arguments

Problem

You want to restart *named* with *ndc*, but keep the same command-line arguments.

Solution

Specify the command-line arguments after the *restart* command. For example:

```
# ndc restart -c /tmp/named.conf
```

Or, if you're not sure what the command-line arguments were, use:

```
# ndc exec
```

The *exec* command tells named to *exec()* a new copy of itself, including any command-line argument it was started with.

Discussion

If you run *ndc* from the command line and *named* is linked against a faulty copy of *getopt()*, you may need to specify "--" as the first argument to *restart* to make sure the options are passed to *named* correctly.

BIND 9 name servers don't support *restart* and *exec*.

See Also

Recipe 3.1, for setting up *ndc* to work with a name server; Recipe 5.4, for a situation in which you'd restart a name server (in this case, to clear the cache); and "Controlling a Name Server" in Chapter 7 of *DNS and BIND*.

5.10 Controlling Multiple named Processes with rndc

Problem

You want to control multiple *named* processes running on the same host with *rndc*.

Solution

Since *rndc* only supports TCP-based communications with name servers, configure the name servers to listen on different addresses for control messages. For example, if your host runs two named processes—one listening on 192.168.0.1 for queries, the other listening on 192.168.0.2—you might configure the first one with this *controls* statement in its *named.conf* file:

```
controls {
    inet 192.168.0.1 allow { localnets; } keys { rndc-key; };
};
```

The second might have this *controls* statement in *named.conf*:

```
controls {
    inet 192.168.0.2 allow { localnets; } keys { rndc-key; };
};
```

If *rndc-key* is *rndc*'s default key, you can control the two *named* processes with:

```
# rndc -s 192.168.0.1
```

Or:

```
# rndc -s 192.168.0.2
```

Discussion

If you want to use different keys to control the two processes, you can add two *server* statements to *rndc.conf*, specifying the proper key to use for each.

You could also set up the two name servers to listen on different control ports, and then use the *port server* substatement in *rndc.conf* to distinguish between the two. For example:

```
server ns1.foo.example {
    port 953;
    key "rndc-key";
};

server ns1-int.foo.example {
    port 1053;
    key "rndc-key";
};
```

This assumes that both *ns1.foo.example* and *ns1-int.foo.example* map to the same address.

See Also

Recipe 3.3 for configuring *rndc* to work with a remote name server using the *rndc.conf*'s *server* statement.

5.11 Controlling Multiple named Processes with ndc

Problem

You want to control multiple *named* processes running on the same host with *ndc*.

Solution

Configure the name servers to create different Unix domain sockets. For example, if the host runs both a caching-only name server and an authoritative-only name server, you might configure a *controls* statement like this one in the caching-only name server's *named.conf* file:

```
controls {
    unix "/var/run/ndc.caching" owner 0 group 0 perm 0660;
};
```

In the other's *named.conf* file, you could add this *controls* statement:

```
controls {
    unix "/var/run/ndc.auth" owner 0 group 0 perm 0660;
};
```

Then, to use *ndc* to control the caching-only name server, run:

```
# ndc -c /var/run/ndc.caching
```

To control the authoritative-only name server, use:

```
# ndc -c /var/run/ndc.auth
```

Discussion

To make this setup a little easier to use, you could create shell aliases from *ndc-caching* and *ndc-auth* to *ndc -c /var/run/ndc.caching* and *ndc -c /var/run/ndc.auth*, respectively.

You can set this up with TCP-based control channels, too, but BIND 8's TCP-based control channels aren't secure. If you opt to use them anyway, see Recipe 5.10 for hints.

See Also

Recipe 5.10 and "Two Name Server in One" in Chapter 11 of *DNS and BIND*.

5.12 Finding Out Who's Querying a Name Server

Problem

You want to find out which resolvers and name servers are querying a name server.

Solution

For BIND 9, turn on query logging with:

```
# rndc querylog
```

Or, for BIND 8:

```
# ndc querylog
```

Then examine the name server's *syslog* output. The name server will log a one-line message each time it receives a query. For BIND 9, the messages look like this:

```
May  4 22:45:14 ns1 named[80090]: client 192.168.0.99#3261: query: www.foo.example IN A
```

This tells us that our name server received a query from the client at 192.168.0.99, port 3261, for A records attached to *www.foo.example* in the Internet class.

On a BIND 8 name server, the messages look like this:

```
May  4 22:53:52 ns1 named[80323]: XX+/192.168.0.99/www.foo.example/A/IN
```

Most of the same information is there, but in a slightly different format: the address the query was received from, the domain name the query asked about, the type of query, and the class of query, separated by slashes. The "XX+" at the beginning indicates that it is a recursive query. Nonrecursive queries show just "XX."

Discussion

Query logging can come in handy if you're trying to track down a problem. However, it generates a lot of output—*quickly*, on a busy name server—so it's probably a bad idea to use all the time. If you're really just interested in how many queries the name server receives, use the name server's statistics instead (Recipes 5.13 and 5.14).

You can also turn on query logging by assigning the logging category *queries* to a particular channel. See Recipe 10.3 for details.

There's no indication in the BIND 9 query logging output of which queries were recursive and which not.

See Also

Recipes 5.13 and 5.14, for measuring the queries a name server receives, and Recipe 10.3, for sending one category of messages to a particular file.

5.13   Measuring a Name Server's Performance

Problem

You want to measure a name server's performance.

Solution

To measure a name server's real performance (that is, the number of queries it answers on an hourly or daily basis), dump statistics periodically and compare the numbers. On a BIND 9.1.0 or later name server, for example, you could use *rndc stats* to dump statistics hourly with this *crontab* entry:

```
0   *   *   *   *    root    rndc stats
```

Every hour, the name server will append data like this to the statistics file (called *named.stats* in the name server's working directory, by default):

```
+++ Statistics Dump +++ (1021327908)
success 5268
referral 57
nxrrset 7938
nxdomain 127
recursion 1946
failure 153
--- Statistics Dump --- (1021327908)
```

Add the values of *success, nxrrset*, and *nxdomain*, and compute the difference between the sums in two successive statistics blocks. Divide by 3600 (seconds) to get the query rate in queries per second.

With BIND 8, you use *ndc stats* to induce the name server to dump statistics, but the name server's statistics look considerably different than BIND 9's. Here's an example:

```
++ Name Server Statistics ++
(Legend)
        RR      RNXD    RFwdR   RDupR   RFail
        RFErr   RErr    RAXFR   RLame   ROpts
        SSysQ   SAns    SFwdQ   SDupQ   SErr
        RQ      RIQ     RFwdQ   RDupQ   RTCP
        SFwdR   SFail   SFErr   SNaAns  SNXD
        RUQ     RURQ    RUXFR   RUUpd
(Global)
        94 0 22 0 0  35 0 0 0 0  7 242727 30 36 0  242744 0 30 0 0  22 0 0 24272
5 0  182058 0 0 0
-- Name Server Statistics --
```

This is just part of the statistics output, printed at the end of each block. The information you need is still there: compute the difference between the values for *SAns* (sent answers) over time to derive the query rate. To find *SAns*, look at the line under

"(Global)". The second number in the third quintet of numbers (242727 in this example) is *SAns*.

Discussion

BIND 9 didn't support dumping statistics until 9.1.0. Of course, you shouldn't be running anything that old, anyway. Here's a quick key to the meaning of the various BIND 9 statistics:

success
> The number of successful queries (those that return a response other than a referral)

referral
> The number of queries that resulted in a referral

nxrrset
> The number of queries for domain names that didn't own the type of record requested

nxdomain
> The number of queries for domain names that didn't exist

recursion
> The number of recursive queries for domain names in the zone that required the name server to send one or more queries

failure
> The number of queries that resulted in a failure other than NXDOMAIN

For an explanation of the many statistics kept by a BIND 8 name server, see "Understanding the BIND Statistics" in Chapter 7 of *DNS and BIND*.

You may also want to test a name server's top-end performance: how quickly it can process queries? There's a program included in the BIND 9 distribution called *queryperf* that helps with that; you'll find it in the *contrib/queryperf* subdirectory. Though it's shipped with BIND 9, it works by sending standard DNS queries, so you can use it to measure the performance of any kind of name server—BIND 9, BIND 8, or "other."

To build it, *cd* to *contrib/queryperf* and run *configure*, then run *make*:

```
$ cd contrib/queryperf
$ ./configure
$ make
```

Next, you need to construct an input file, telling *queryperf* what queries to send to the name server. Each line in the input file must contain a domain name and a type to look up:

```
www.foo.example A
foo.example SOA
```

(The class is assumed to be *IN*, for Internet. If you want to measure a name server's performance in processing Hesiod queries, you're on your own. You're also a weirdo.)

If you want to test a name server's performance answering queries for authoritative zone data, use domain names in zones that the name server is authoritative for. If you want to test a name server's performance resolving queries that require recursion, use domain names outside of the name server's authoritative zones. Also, make sure you choose lots of different domain names, or the name server will quickly cache the answers and you won't get a representative measurement of performance.

Once you've created the input file, run *queryperf*. Use the *−d* command-line option to specify the name of the input file. You can specify how long (in seconds) you want the test to run with *−l*, or that you want to go through the list of queries just once with *−1*. If you give *queryperf* a time limit and the program exhausts the queries in the input file before the test is over, it'll start again at the beginning. The *−s* and *−p* options allow you to specify the server and port you want to query, respectively. The defaults are the local host and port 53. For other command-line options, run *queryperf* with an option it doesn't understand, like *−?*.

Here's a sample run of *queryperf*:

```
$ queryperf -d input/foo.example -l 60

DNS Query Performance Testing Tool
Version: $Id: queryperf.c,v 1.1.1.2.2.1 2001/09/27 00.44.26 marka Exp $

[Status] Processing input data
[Status] Sending queries
[Status] Testing complete

Statistics:

  Parse input file:     multiple times
  Run time limit:       60 seconds
  Ran through file:     0 times

  Queries sent:         265935 queries
  Queries completed:    265935 queries
  Queries lost:         0 queries

  Percentage completed: 100.00%
  Percentage lost:        0.00%

  Started at:           Mon May 13 16:26:28 2002
  Finished at:          Mon May 13 16:27:28 2002
  Ran for:              60.458815 seconds

  Queries per second:   4398.614164 qps
```

This was a very short test—60 seconds—of queries for domain names in zones my name server is authoritative for, but the performance is impressive nonetheless: nearly 4,400 queries per second.

Note that you probably don't want to run a stress test like this on a production name server during work hours. You may even want to run the name server you're testing on an alternate port, as described in Recipe 3.25.

See Also

Recipe 3.25, "Understanding the BIND Statistics" in Chapter 7 of *DNS and BIND*, and "Capacity Planning" in Chapter 8.

5.14 Measuring Queries for Records in Particular Zones

Problem

You want to measure the number of queries a name server receives for records in zones it is authoritative for.

Solution

Use the BIND 9 *zone-statistics* substatement. To measure the statistics for just a few zones, use *zone-statistics* as a *zone* substatement. For example:

```
zone "foo.example" {
    type slave;
    masters { 192.168.0.1; };
    file "bak.foo.example";
    zone-statistics yes;
};
```

To keep statistics for all zones, use *zone-statistics* as an *options* substatement:

```
options {
    directory "/var/named";
    zone-statistics yes;
};
```

Then, to dump the zone's statistics, use *rndc stats*. The statistics are written to the file *named.stats* in the name server's working directory, by default. Here's a short sample of a *named.stats* file:

```
+++ Statistics Dump +++ (1020821387)
success 37
referral 0
nxrrset 60
```

```
nxdomain 9
recursion 12
failure 6
success 6 foo.example
referral 0 foo.example
nxrrset 3 foo.example
nxdomain 1 foo.example
recursion 0 foo.example
failure 0 foo.example
--- Statistics Dump --- (1020821387)
```

The first six counters are global: total counts for the name server since it started. The next six are specific to the *foo.example* zone. The sum of the zone-specific values for *success*, *nxrrset*, and *nxdomain* is the total number of queries for records in the zone. (*nxrrset* is a count of queries for types of records that didn't exist, while *nxdomain* counts queries for domain names that didn't exist).

Discussion

There's no mechanism comparable to *zone-statistics* in BIND 8. While you could turn on query logging and extrapolate the same statistics, the overhead would be considerable.

Speaking of overhead, the zone statistics mechanism does use a little extra memory on the name server to store the counters.

See Also

Recipe 5.12 for information on query logging, which can tell you who is querying a name server; and Recipe 5.13, for measuring aggregate performance.

5.15   Monitoring a Name Server

Problem

You want to monitor a zone's name servers.

Solution

Use a freely available package that supports monitoring name servers. The well-thought-of *mon* supports monitoring the DNS service. You can get a copy from *http://www.kernel.org/software/mon/*. Since the DNS-monitoring portion of the package, *dns.monitor*, is written in Perl using the Net::DNS module, it's easy to adapt to your particular needs.

Discussion

You can also use Dave Barr's excellent *dnswalk*, available from *http://www.visi.com/~barr/dnswalk/*, for DNS monitoring. Also built using Net::DNS, *dnswalk* detects lame and unresponsive name servers, as well as many common zone data errors. Just make sure *dnswalk* can transfer a copy of the zone you want to monitor, and specify *dnswalk*'s *−l* command-line option to turn on lame delegation checking. Then you can run *dnswalk* periodically from *cron* and send yourself the output.

See Also

Recipes 9.7 through 9.10 for examples of programming with Net::DNS.

5.16 Limiting Concurrent Zone Transfers

Problem

You want to limit the number of concurrent zone transfers a name server will allow.

Solution

On a BIND 9 master name server, use the *transfers-out options* substatement. For example:

```
options {
    directory "/var/named";
    transfers-out 4;
};
```

This limits the number of zone transfers the master will serve concurrently. The default limit is 10. Unfortunately, BIND 8 name servers don't support *transfers-out*.

On a slave name server, use the *transfers-in options* substatement. For example:

```
options {
    directory "/var/named";
    transfers-in 4;
};
```

This limits the number of concurrent zone transfers the slave will request from its master name servers. The default is also 10.

Discussion

There's another *options* substatement available for limiting the number of concurrent zone transfers a slave name server will request from any one master: *transfers-per-ns*.

The default value for *transfers-per-ns* is two, and you can override the limit for particular name servers using the *transfers* substatement of the *server* statement. For example:

```
server 10.0.0.1 {
    transfers 10;
};
```

If you limit the number of concurrent zone transfers too aggressively, it may take the slave name server longer to converge with its master. For example, if the slave can only start 2 concurrent zone transfers from its master but needs to transfer 10 zones, it'll start 2, wait until 1 completes, start another, and so on, until all 10 have transferred. That will probably take more time than just starting all 10 at once.

Conversely, allowing too many concurrent zone transfers soaks up a lot of resources on both master and slave name servers.

See Also

Recipe 5.17, for limiting the number of TCP clients of any kind a name server will serve; and "Zone Transfers" in Chapter 10 of *DNS and BIND*.

5.17   Limiting Concurrent TCP Clients

Problem

You want to limit the number of concurrent TCP clients a name server handles.

Solution

Use the BIND 9 *tcp-clients options* substatement. For example:

```
options {
    directory "/var/named";
    tcp-clients 500;
};
```

The default limit is 100 TCP clients.

Discussion

The limit on TCP clients applies to both discrete TCP queries and TCP zone transfers. A name server probably won't receive many TCP-based queries from resolvers, since nearly all resolvers send UDP-based queries by default. Most zone transfer requests, however, are TCP-based so don't set the limit lower than *transfers-out*.

Remember that the operating system places a limit on the number of file descriptors available to the *named* process, and each TCP connection to the name server uses one of these. If you make the *tcp-clients* limit higher than the OS-imposed limit, it's possible the name server will run out of file descriptors, which it needs for reading and writing zone data files and listening for control messages.

If a name server reaches the limit on TCP clients, it will refuse those TCP-based queries and you'll see messages like this one in its *syslog* output:

```
named[579]: client 192.168.0.11#1567: no more TCP clients: quota reached
```

Check whether the TCP queries the name server is serving are legitimate (e.g., not part of some distributed denial of service attack). If they are, raise the limit to accommodate them.

There's no corresponding substatement in BIND 8.

See Also

Recipe 5.16, for limiting concurrent zone transfers.

5.18   Limiting Concurrent Recursive Clients

Problem

You want to limit the number of concurrent recursive clients a name server handles.

Solution

Use the BIND 9 *recursive-clients options* substatement. For example:

```
options {
    directory "/var/named";
    recursive-clients 500;
};
```

The default limit is 1,000 recursive clients.

Discussion

With *recursive-clients*, you can limit the number of recursive queriers a name server will handle concurrently. A name server receives recursive queries both from resolvers and from name servers that use it as a forwarder. Since each recursive query consumes about 20K of memory, the total amount of memory needed to service 1,000 queriers—the default limit—is about 20MB. If a name server doesn't have that much real memory available, you may need to set its limit lower.

If a name server reaches this limit, it will refuse further recursive queries and you'll see messages like this one in its *syslog* output:

```
named[579]: client 192.168.0.11#1567: no more recursive clients: quota reached
```

Check whether the recursive clients the name server is serving are legitimate (e.g., not part of some distributed denial of service attack). If they are, and there's sufficient memory available on the host, raise the limit to accommodate them.

There's no corresponding substatement in BIND 8.

See Also

"Resource Limits" in Chapter 10 of *DNS and BIND*.

5.19   Dynamically Updating a Zone

Problem

You want to dynamically update a zone.

Solution

Use the *nsupdate* program to send updates to your zone. First, start *nsupdate* in interactive mode:

```
$ nsupdate
```

The basic command in *nsupdate*'s interactive mode is *update*. To add a new record, use *update add*. To delete one or more records, use *update delete*. *update add* takes a resource record, including an explicit TTL, as an argument. For example:

```
> update add host.foo.example. 3600 A 192.168.0.31
```

You can leave out the class, though; it defaults to *IN*, for "Internet."

To delete a particular record, specify the record as an argument to *update delete*:

```
> update delete foo.example. MX 10 mail.foo.example.
```

To delete all records of a particular type attached to a domain name, specify the domain name and type as an argument to *update delete*:

```
> update delete foo.example. MX
```

Finally, to delete all records of any type attached to a domain name, specify just the domain name as an argument to *update delete*:

```
> update delete host.foo.example.
```

You can perform more than one add or delete operation at once by specifying multiple *update* commands, each on its own line, as long as the changes are made to a single zone. Once you're ready to send the update, type:

```
> send
```

If you're running a BIND 8 version of *nsupdate*, just type a blank line:

```
>
```

Discussion

Here's a complete *nsupdate* session:

```
$ nsupdate
> update delete www.foo.example. IN A
> update add www.foo.example. 3600 IN A 192.168.0.89
> send
```

nsupdate can communicate with (and hence update) any name server. It looks up the SOA record of the zone the domain name in the update belongs in and sends the update to the name server listed in the MNAME field. Consequently, you should make sure the MNAME field of each of your zones' SOA records contains the domain name of the real primary master name server for the zone.

Since *nsupdate* gives you very little feedback, you may find it helpful to run *nsupdate* with the *−d* (debug) option. That way, you can see the output from the name server that receives the update.

See Also

nsupdate(8); Recipe 3.10, for how to allow dynamic updates to a zone; Recipes 5.20, 5.21, and 5.22 for variations on sending dynamic updates to a name server; Recipes 9.9 and 9.10, for sending dynamic updates programmatically; and "DNS Dynamic Update" in Chapter 10 of *DNS and BIND*.

5.20 Sending Dynamic Updates to a Particular Name Server

Problem

You want to send a dynamic update to a particular name server, possibly not the one in the MNAME field of the zone's SOA record.

Solution

Use the BIND 9 version of *nsupdate* and specify the name server you want to send the update to as the argument to the *server* command. Then specify the update with an *update* command. For example:

```
$ nsupdate
> server ns2.foo.example.
> update delete foo.example. TXT
> update add foo.example. 3600 TXT "This is a test record"
> send
```

Discussion

nsupdate continues to send updates to the specified name server until you designate a different name server with another *server* command or exit.

The BIND 8 version of *nsupdate* doesn't support the *server* command, but you can use a BIND 9 *nsupdate* with a BIND 8 name server. In fact, you can use *nsupdate* with any name server that supports dynamic update. Dynamic update messages have a standard format, after all.

You can use an IP address as the argument to *server*, too.

See Also

nsupdate(8).

5.21 Setting Prerequisites in a Dynamic Update

Problem

You want to set a prerequisite in a dynamic update.

Solution

Use *nsupdate* and specify the prerequisite you want as an argument to the *prereq* command. Then specify the update with an *update* command. *nsupdate* supports the following kinds of prerequisites:

nxdomain
> The following domain name doesn't exist.

yxdomain
> The following domain name exists.

nxrrset
> The following domain name doesn't own records of the specified type.

yxrrset
> The following domain name owns records of the specified type. If the RDATA is specified, it must match, too.

For example, you could use this *nsupdate* command to add an A record to *foo.example* only if *foo.example* doesn't already have an A record:

```
$ nsupdate
> prereq nxrrset foo.example A
> update add foo.example. 3600 A 192.168.0.86
> send
```

In order to change *www.foo.example's* A record to 192.168.0.86 only if it's currently 192.168.0.99, you could use:

```
$ nsupdate
> prereq yxrrset www.foo.example A 192.168.0.99
> update delete www.foo.example A 192.168.0.99
> update add www.foo.example 3600 A 192.168.0.86
> send
```

Discussion

Remember that the BIND 8 version of *nsupdate* doesn't support the *send* command. Instead, just type a blank line.

See Also

nsupdate(8) and "DNS Dynamic Update" in Chapter 10 of *DNS and BIND*.

5.22   Sending TSIG-Signed Dynamic Updates

Problem

You want to send a TSIG-signed dynamic update.

Solution

Use *nsupdate's* *–k* command-line option or the *key* command in *nsupdate's* interactive mode.

The *–k* command-line option takes as an argument the path to a file that contains a TSIG key, as generated by the *dnssec-keygen* program. Those files have names of the form *Kkey-name.+157+number.key*. For example:

```
$ nsupdate -k Kdhcp-server.foo.example.+157+27656.key
```

nsupdate's *key* command takes the name of a TSIG key and the base 64 representation of the key data (just like in a *key* statement) as arguments. For example:

```
$ nsupdate
> key dhcp-server.foo.example CPB4fRniZYUPobYF/4igZg==
> update delete foo.example. NS ns1.foo.example.
> send
```

Discussion

Remember that the name of the key, not just the key data, needs to match in *nsupdate* and in the name server's configuration.

BIND 8's version of *nsupdate* doesn't support the *key* command (yet another reason to use BIND 9's *nsupdate*). Also, the syntax of the argument to *–k* is different: *key-directory:key-name*. For example:

```
$ nsupdate -k /var/named:dhcp-server.foo.example
```

Note that the BIND 8 *nsupdate* really doesn't like key files generated with BIND 9's *dnssec-keygen*; use BIND 8's *dnskeygen* instead.

Finally, BIND 9's *nsupdate* also supports a *–y* option, which takes as arguments the name of the key and the key data, as in:

```
$ nsupdate -y dhcp-server.foo.example:CPB4fRniZYUPobYF/4igZg==
```

Using the *–y* option is a bad idea on any host on which unauthorized users have accounts, since the key name and data are visible to anyone who can run *ps*.

See Also

nsupdate(8); Recipe 3.10, for allowing TSIG-signed dynamic updates to a zone; and Recipe 9.10, for sending TSIG-signed updates programmatically.

5.23   Setting Up a Backup Primary Master Name Server

Problem

You want to establish a "backup" primary master name server, to assume the responsibilities of the regular primary master name server, should it fail.

Solution

Configure slave name servers with the address of the regular primary master name server first in their *masters* substatements, then with the address of the backup primary master. For example, if you wanted to designate 192.168.0.2 as the backup primary master name server, you could use *zone* statements like this one:

```
zone "foo.example" {
    type slave;
    masters {
        192.168.0.1;    // regular primary master
        192.168.0.2;    // backup primary master
    };
    file "bak.foo.example";
};
```

The backup primary master should serve as a slave when everything's functioning correctly. (But be sure to configure the backup primary master to allow zone transfers to the other slaves.) Then, if the regular primary master fails, you can follow the instructions in Recipe 5.24 to turn the backup primary master name server into a full-fledged primary master.

Discussion

Most versions of BIND contact the first name server in the *masters* list first. They only query the second name server if the first one doesn't respond—because it's crashed, for example—or if there's an error in the response. As long as the regular, workaday primary master continues responding, they'll transfer the zone from it.

BIND 8 name servers from 8.2 on query all of the name servers listed in the *masters* substatement, and transfer the zone from the one that replies with the highest serial number (if there's a tie, the one earliest in the list). That will still work when the normal primary master is running, and if it fails, the name servers get their zone transfers from the backup.

See Also

Recipe 5.24 for instructions on what to do when a primary master name server fails.

5.24 Promoting a Slave Name Server to the Primary Master

Problem

You want to "promote" a slave name server to be the primary master name server.

Solution

Change the *zone* statement for the zones you want the slave to be primary master for from *type slave* to *type master*, and delete the *masters* substatements. For example, this *zone* statement:

```
zone "foo.example" {
    type slave;
    masters { 192.68.0.1; };
    file "bak.foo.example";
};
```

Becomes this *zone* statement:

```
zone "foo.example" {
    type master;
    file "bak.foo.example";
};
```

If you allow dynamic updates to any of the zones, change the MNAME field of those zones' SOA records to the domain name of the new primary and add an *allow-update* or *update-policy* substatement. For example:

```
zone "foo.example" {
    type master;
    file "bak.foo.example";
    allow-update { 192.168.0.1; };
};
```

If you restricted zone transfers from the old primary, duplicate the *allow-transfer* substatement from the old *zone* statement.

Then reload the name server with *rndc reload* or *ndc reload*, as appropriate.

If you followed the instructions in Recipe 5.23 and set up the slaves to use this name server as their backup master, you're done. If not, you'll need to reconfigure your slaves to use the new primary as their master. Just change the IP address in the *masters* substatement to the address of the new primary and reload.

Discussion

If you're so inclined, you can rename the zone data file to fit your standard for primary master zones. For example, we might rename *bak.foo.example* to *db.foo.example*.

Check the *zone* statement on the old primary master for other substatements that you might need to duplicate on the new primary master, such as *also-notify* and *check-names*.

See Also

Recipe 5.23 and "Coping with Disaster" in Chapter 8 of *DNS and BIND*.

5.25 Running Multiple Primary Master Name Servers for the Same Zone

Problem

You want to run more than one primary master name server for the same zone.

Solution

Configure multiple name servers with *zone* statements of *type master* for the zone, then use a program such as *scp*, *rdist*, or *rsync* to keep the zone data files synchronized.

Discussion

An *rdist distfile* to synchronize zone data files between two name servers might look like this:

```
DUPS = ( ns2.foo.example ns3.foo.example )

FILES = ( /var/named/db.foo.example )

${FILES} -> ${DUPS}

    install;
    special "rndc reload foo.example";
```

A scheme like this won't work with a dynamically updated zone, because the zone data file won't usually be rewritten right away after the name server receives an update. Moreover, if more than one primary master actually accepts dynamic updates, *rsync*-style synchronization might corrupt the zone data file.

See Also

rdist(1) and *scp(1)*.

5.26   Creating a Zone Programmatically

Problem

You want to create a new zone on a name server programmatically.

Solution

Create a minimal zone data file that uses only relative domain names in the owner field of the records. For example:

```
$TTL 86400
@    IN    SOA    ns1.foo.example.    hostmaster.foo.example.    (
     2002051200
     3600
     900
     604800
     3600 )

     IN    NS    ns1.foo.example.
     IN    NS    ns2.foo.example.

     IN    A     10.0.0.1

     IN    MX    10 mail.foo.example.

www IN    CNAME    @
```

Then write a script to add a new *zone* statement to the name server's *named.conf* file, referring to the zone data file. Finally, use *rndc reconfig* or *ndc reconfig*, as appropriate, to tell the name server to reread *named.conf*.

An example script, *addzone.pl*, is included in the tar file that accompanies this book (see the Preface for details). To run *addzone.pl*, specify the domain name of the zone and the name of the minimal zone data file as arguments:

```
# addzone.pl baz.example db.template
```

Discussion

addzone.pl is fairly simple-minded: it assumes its working directory is the name server's working directory. And I'm sure some Perl hacker could replace it with a single-line script.

See Also

Recipe 1.15 for configuring a name server as the primary master for a zone, and Recipe 5.6 for adding a zone without restarting the name server.

5.27 Migrating from One Domain Name to Another

Problem

You need to migrate from one domain name to another because you're changing the name of your zone.

Solution

Once you've established the new zone, create aliases pointing from each domain name in the old zone to the corresponding domain name in the new zone. For example:

```
a.foo.example.    IN    CNAME    a.bar.example.
b.foo.example.    IN    CNAME    b.bar.example.
c.d.foo.example.  IN    CNAME    c.d.bar.example.
```

Change the NS and MX records in the old zone, as necessary, so they don't point to aliases:

```
foo.example.    IN    NS    ns1.bar.example.
                IN    NS    ns2.bar.example.
                IN    MX    10 mail.bar.example.
```

Change the PTR records for these hosts to reverse-map to their new domain names, too:

```
20.0.168.192.in-addr.arpa.    IN    PTR    a.bar.example.
21.0.168.192.in-addr.arpa.    IN    PTR    b.bar.example.
22.0.168.192.in-addr.arpa.    IN    PTR    c.d.bar.example.
```

Next, configure any resolvers that use the old domain name as their local domain name to use the new one; for example:

```
domain bar.example
```

This may require additional changes to the configuration of the host. If the host runs a mailer or a web server, check the server's configuration files. You may need to change the domain name the mailer uses in return addresses or the domain name it sees as local. You may need to reconfigure the web server with its new domain name or install a new SSL server certificate. Also, check that any authorization files refer to the new domain names, since IP addresses will now reverse-map to them.

Wait for some grace period, and then remove the aliases and the old zone. If you're not sure how long to keep the old zone around, you can use the zone statistics described in Recipe 5.14 to determine whether the aliases are still being used.

Discussion

If you run BIND 9 name servers for the zone, you may be able to use the new DNAME record to simplify the setup of the old zone. DNAME records work like substitution rules in *sed* or Perl. For example, this DNAME record will "synthesize" CNAME records aliasing each domain name in *foo.example* to the corresponding domain name in *bar.example*:

```
foo.example.    IN    DNAME    bar.example.
```

A querier looking up *a.foo.example* will find this CNAME record, created on the fly from the DNAME record:

```
a.foo.example.    IN    CNAME    a.bar.example.
```

While a querier looking up *c.d.foo.example* will have this CNAME record returned:

```
c.d.foo.example.    IN    CNAME    c.d.bar.example.
```

See Also

Recipe 2.3 for creating individual aliases using CNAME records, Recipe 5.14 for measuring zone statistics, and Recipes 9.2 and 9.3 for configuration of a resolver's local domain name.

## CHAPTER 6

Delegation and Registration

6.0   Introduction

As the administrator of one or more zones, you need to manage two kinds of delegation: from your zones' parent zones to your zone, and from your zones to their subdomains. Both are ongoing processes:

- After registering a domain name (as in Recipe 1.5), you still must update the delegation any time the set of authoritative name servers changes. Recipes 6.6 and 6.7 describe ways of handling this as painlessly as possible.

- After delegating a subdomain of your zone to a set of name servers, you must check the delegation periodically (Recipe 6.5) to make sure the delegation remains correct.

You also need to manage this delegation for two kinds of zones: forward- and reverse-mapping zones. Delegating reverse-mapping subdomains that correspond to a network or subnet involves more than you might expect. It's covered in Recipes 6.3 and 6.4.

6.1   Delegating a Subdomain

Problem

You want to delegate a subdomain of your zone to a set of name servers.

Solution

Add NS records to your zone's data file delegating the subdomain to the name servers. For example, to delegate the *baz.bar.example* subdomain to the name servers *ns1.baz.bar.example* and *ns2.foo.example*, you'd add these two NS records to the *bar.example* zone data file:

```
baz.bar.example.    IN    NS    ns1.baz.bar.example.
baz.bar.example.    IN    NS    ns2.foo.example.
```

In this example, you'll also need to add an A record for *ns1.baz.bar.example*, even though the name server's A record would normally appear in the *baz.bar.example* zone:

```
ns1.baz.bar.example.   IN   A   10.0.1.1
```

Without the A record—called a *glue record*—another name server that was referred to *ns1.baz.bar.example* would not be able to follow the referral, since in order to find *ns1.baz.bar.example*'s address, it would need to query *ns1.baz.bar.example*. That's like trying to find someone's telephone number by calling and asking.

Discussion

The simplest test for determining whether you need to include a name server's A record with delegation is to check whether the domain name of the name server ends in the domain name of the subdomain being delegated to it. If so, you need to include an A record for the name server.

The name servers that the subdomain is delegated to need a zone data file for the subdomain and a *zone* statement configuring them as authoritative for the zone. So, on *ns1.baz.bar.example* and *ns2.foo.example*, you'd expect to find a *zone* statement like this:

```
zone "baz.bar.example" {
    type master;
    file "db.baz.bar.example";
};
```

Of course, one of the name servers is probably a slave for *baz.bar.example*.

See Also

Recipes 1.15 and 1.16, for instructions on configuring a primary master and a slave name server for a zone, and "How to Become a Parent: Creating Subdomains" in Chapter 9 of *DNS and BIND*.

6.2   Delegating a Subdomain of a Reverse-Mapping Zone

Problem

You want to delegate a subdomain of your reverse-mapping zone to a set of name servers.

Solution

Just as with a forward-mapping zone, add NS records to your reverse-mapping zone's data file delegating the subdomain to the name servers. For example, to

delegate the *1.168.192.in-addr.arpa* subdomain to the name servers *ns1.baz.bar.
example* and *ns2.foo.example*, you'd add these two NS records to the *168.192.in-
addr.arpa* zone data file:

```
1.168.192.in-addr.arpa.    IN   NS   ns1.baz.bar.example.
1.168.192.in-addr.arpa.    IN   NS   ns2.foo.example.
```

Discussion

There's very little difference between delegating a subdomain of a forward-mapping
zone and a subdomain of a reverse-mapping zone: you add NS records to the parent
zone, specifying the name of the subdomain and the domain names of the name servers. Some of the labels in the subdomain's name are the octets in an IP address, but
the name server doesn't care about that.

The correspondence between octets and labels causes problems if you use network
or subnet masks that don't break on an octet boundary—you end up with either
multiple zones per network or subnet or multiple networks per zone. For more, see
Recipes 6.3 and 6.4.

Oh, there is one difference in delegating reverse-mapping zones: glue A records are
rarely necessary in reverse-mapping zones, since most people don't give their name
servers names like *ns1.1.168.192.in-addr.arpa*.

See Also

Recipes 6.3 and 6.4, for delegating reverse mapping for networks with network or
subnet masks that don't break on an octet boundary.

6.3 Delegating Reverse-Mapping for Networks with Non-Octet Masks

Problem

You want to delegate responsibility for reverse-mapping a network's IP addresses to
a set of name servers, but the network mask or subnet mask doesn't fall on an octet
boundary.

Solution

Determine how many reverse-mapping zones correspond to the network. Here's a
table to show you how many you'll have.

Size of network	Number of reverse-mapping
/9	128 reverse-mapping zones such as *2.1.in-addr.arpa*
/10	64 ""

Size of network	Number of reverse-mapping
/11	32 ""
/12	16 ""
/13	8 ""
/14	4 ""
/15	2 ""
/17	128 reverse-mapping zones such as *3.2.1.in-addr.arpa*
/18	64 ""
/19	32 ""
/20	16 ""
/21	8 ""
/22	4 ""
/23	2 ""
/25–32	See Recipe 6.4

For example, say your network is 10/8 and you want to delegate the reverse-mapping zones for the subnet 10.192/10 to your European subsidiary's name servers. That subnetwork corresponds to 64 reverse-mapping zones, from *192.10.in-addr.arpa* to *255.10.in-addr.arpa*. That's a lot of delegation to add to the *10.in-addr.arpa* zone data file: if each zone has two name servers, that's 128 NS records!

BIND name servers give you a shortcut, though. You can use the *$GENERATE* control statement to add a group of records that differ only by a number. For example, if your European subsidiary's name servers are called *ns1.eu.corp.example* and *ns2.eu.corp.example*, you could delegate all 64 reverse-mapping zones to them with just these two *$GENERATE* control statements:

```
$GENERATE 192-255 $ NS ns1.eu.corp.example.
$GENERATE 192-255 $ NS ns2.eu.corp.example.
```

Discussion

Unfortunately, there's no corresponding way to generate the *zone* statements you'll need on the name servers the zones are delegated to. You'd need a full 64 *zone* statements in each name server's *named.conf* file.

See Also

Recipe 6.4 for handling networks smaller than a /24, and "Subnetting on a Non-Octet Boundary" in Chapter 9 of *DNS and BIND*.

6.4   Delegating Reverse-Mapping for Networks Smaller than a /24

Problem

You want to delegate responsibility for reverse-mapping a network's IP addresses to a set of name servers, but the network or subnet is smaller than a /24.

Solution

Add CNAME records to the domain names that would normally own PTR records, making those domain names aliases to domain names in other zones. Those zones can be either new zones or existing zones. If they are new zones, delegate the zones to the appropriate name servers. If they are existing zones, make sure they're already delegated to the proper name servers.

Here's an example. Say you manage *0.168.192.in-addr.arpa*, the reverse-mapping zone for the network 192.168.0/24. You have divided it into two subnets, though: 192.168.0.0/25 and 192.168.0.128/25. You'd like to delegate responsibility for maintaining each subnet's reverse-mapping information to a different set of name servers, but you've only got a single reverse-mapping zone, *0.168.192.in-addr.arpa*.

So you add CNAME records to the zone data file for *0.168.192.in-addr.arpa*. In addition, the administrator of the first subnet, 192.168.0.0/25, wants a new subdomain, *0-127.0.168.192.in-addr.arpa*, delegated to his name servers. The administrator of the 192.168.0.128/25 subnet has an existing zone, *bar.example*, and he'd like to manage just that zone.

For the first subnet, you add CNAME records like these:

```
1.0.168.192.in-addr.arpa.    IN    CNAME    1.0-127.0.168.192.in-addr.arpa.
2.0.168.192.in-addr.arpa.    IN    CNAME    2.0-127.0.168.192.in-addr.arpa.
```

For the second subnet, you add CNAME records like these:

```
129.0.168.192.in-addr.arpa.    IN    CNAME    129.0.168.192.bar.example.
130.0.168.192.in-addr.arpa.    IN    CNAME    130.0.168.192.bar.example.
```

Since the *0-127.0.168.192.in-addr.arpa* subdomain is new, you'll also need to add delegation to the *0.168.192.in-addr.arpa* zone data file:

```
0-127.0.168.192.in-addr.arpa.    IN    NS    ns1.foo.example.
0-127.0.168.192.in-addr.arpa.    IN    NS    ns2.foo.example.
```

On *ns1.foo.example* and *ns2.foo.example*, the administrator would add *zone* statements like this one:

```
zone "0-127.0.168.192.in-addr.arpa" {
    type master;
    file "db.192.168.0.0-127";
};
```

And within the zone data file for *0-127.0.168.192.in-addr.arpa*, he'd add PTR records like these:

```
1.0-127.0.168.192.in-addr.arpa.    IN    PTR    ns1.foo.example.
2.0-127.0.168.192.in-addr.arpa.    IN    PTR    mail.foo.example.
```

The administrator of the second subnet can add PTR records like these to the zone data file for *bar.example*:

```
129.0.168.192.bar.example.    IN    PTR    monkey.bar.example.
130.0.168.192.bar.example.    IN    PTR    martini.bar.example.
```

Discussion

This scheme is fairly simple, although its simplicity is obscured by all the nasty syntax. Basically, where you'd normally add PTR records in the *0.168.192.in-addr.arpa* zone, you add CNAME records that create aliases to domain names in other zones. Then, at the domain names those aliases point to, you attach PTR records. A name server looking up a PTR record for *2.0.168.192.in-addr.arpa*, for example, will find that that domain name is an alias for *2.0-127.0.168.192.in-addr.arpa*, and on a successive lookup will find the PTR record attached to *2.0-127.0.168.192.in-addr.arpa*.

If you need to create lots of very similar CNAME records, avail yourself of the *$GENERATE* control statement, introduced back in Recipe 2.20. For example, you could create CNAME records for all of the 192.168.0.0/25 network with just this control statement:

```
$GENERATE 1-127 $ CNAME $.0-127.0.168.192.in-addr.arpa.
```

The naming scheme I used for the new zone, *0-127.0.168.192.in-addr.arpa*, reflects both the values of the first three octets of the reverse-mapped addresses (192.168.0) and the range of values in the fourth octet (0 to 127). This scheme is just a useful convention, though; there's nothing magic about it. If you prefer a different scheme, you're welcome to use it.

See Also

Recipe 2.20, for the syntax of the *$GENERATE* control statement; RFC 2317, the official description of the technique; and "Subnetting on a Non-Octet Boundary" in Chapter 9 of *DNS and BIND*.

6.5   Checking Delegation

Problem

You need to check the delegation of a zone.

Solution

There are several ways to check a zone's delegation. One of the easiest is to use the *+trace* option supported by the BIND 9 version of *dig*. When you specify *+trace*, *dig* begins by looking up NS records for the root zone, using the local name server, and then sends a nonrecursive query to one of the root name servers. It continues by following referrals to other name servers until it finds the answer to the question specified on the command line. Here's an example:

```
$ dig +trace cnn.com

; <<>> DiG 9.2.1 <<>> +trace cnn.com
;; global options:  printcmd
.                          516931  IN      NS      A.ROOT-SERVERS.NET.
.                          516931  IN      NS      B.ROOT-SERVERS.NET.
.                          516931  IN      NS      C.ROOT-SERVERS.NET.
.                          516931  IN      NS      D.ROOT-SERVERS.NET.
.                          516931  IN      NS      E.ROOT-SERVERS.NET.
.                          516931  IN      NS      F.ROOT-SERVERS.NET.
.                          516931  IN      NS      G.ROOT-SERVERS.NET.
.                          516931  IN      NS      H.ROOT-SERVERS.NET.
.                          516931  IN      NS      I.ROOT-SERVERS.NET.
.                          516931  IN      NS      J.ROOT-SERVERS.NET.
.                          516931  IN      NS      K.ROOT-SERVERS.NET.
.                          516931  IN      NS      L.ROOT-SERVERS.NET.
.                          516931  IN      NS      M.ROOT-SERVERS.NET.
;; Received 292 bytes from 192.168.0.1#53(192.168.0.1) in 13 ms

com.                       172800  IN      NS      A.GTLD-SERVERS.NET.
com.                       172800  IN      NS      G.GTLD-SERVERS.NET.
com.                       172800  IN      NS      H.GTLD-SERVERS.NET.
com.                       172800  IN      NS      C.GTLD-SERVERS.NET.
com.                       172800  IN      NS      I.GTLD-SERVERS.NET.
com.                       172800  IN      NS      B.GTLD-SERVERS.NET.
com.                       172800  IN      NS      D.GTLD-SERVERS.NET.
com.                       172800  IN      NS      L.GTLD-SERVERS.NET.
com.                       172800  IN      NS      F.GTLD-SERVERS.NET.
com.                       172800  IN      NS      J.GTLD-SERVERS.NET.
com.                       172800  IN      NS      K.GTLD-SERVERS.NET.
com.                       172800  IN      NS      E.GTLD-SERVERS.NET.
com.                       172800  IN      NS      M.GTLD-SERVERS.NET.
;; Received 457 bytes from 198.41.0.4#53(A.ROOT-SERVERS.NET) in 80 ms

cnn.com.                   172800  IN      NS      TWDNS-01.NS.AOL.com.
cnn.com.                   172800  IN      NS      TWDNS-02.NS.AOL.com.
cnn.com.                   172800  IN      NS      TWDNS-03.NS.AOL.com.
cnn.com.                   172800  IN      NS      TWDNS-04.NS.AOL.com.
;; Received 188 bytes from 192.5.6.30#53(A.GTLD-SERVERS.NET) in 78 ms

cnn.com.                   300     IN      A       64.236.24.4
cnn.com.                   300     IN      A       64.236.24.12
```

```
cnn.com.              300   IN   A    64.236.16.20
cnn.com.              300   IN   A    64.236.16.52
cnn.com.              300   IN   A    64.236.24.20
cnn.com.              300   IN   A    64.236.24.28
cnn.com.              300   IN   A    64.236.16.84
cnn.com.              300   IN   A    64.236.16.116
cnn.com.              600   IN   NS   twdns-01.ns.aol.com.
cnn.com.              600   IN   NS   twdns-02.ns.aol.com.
cnn.com.              600   IN   NS   twdns-03.ns.aol.com.
cnn.com.              600   IN   NS   twdns-04.ns.aol.com.
;; Received 316 bytes from 149.174.213.151#53(TWDNS-01.NS.AOL.com) in 123 ms
```

After discovering the root name servers list, the instance of *dig* queried *a.root-servers.net* for A records for *cnn.com*, then followed a referral to one of the *com* name servers, *a.gtld-servers.net*, and then followed another referral to one of the *cnn.com* name servers, *twdns-01.ns.aol.com*. This traces the iterative name resolution process an external name server would use to resolve *cnn.com* domain names. The fact that it succeeded shows that the delegation from the *com* zone's name servers (one of them, anyway) to *cnn.com* works.

Discussion

The tools *dnswalk* and *doc* also check delegation. *dnswalk* checks delegation to subdomains of the zone you designate on the command line if you use the –*l* option— but it needs to transfer the zone to check it, so don't bother running a command like:

```
$ dnswalk com.
```

However, it's very useful if you want to check the delegations below your zone.

doc, which is included in the BIND 8 *tar* file of contributed utilities (available in the same directory as the BIND 8 source code—see Recipe 1.11 for details), also checks delegation to a zone's name servers, as well as synchronization between those name servers and their parent name servers.

See Also

Recipe 1.11 for instructions on how to get the BIND 8 source code (as well as the contributed utilities), and Recipe 5.15 for how to get *dnswalk*.

6.6   Moving a Name Server

Problem

You want to move a name server to another address.

Solution

If you have three or more authoritative name servers registered with your registrar, remove the one you'll move well ahead of the change. This entails removing the NS record pointing to the name server in your zone data and using your registrar's interface to request that they remove the NS record delegating the zone to the name server from the parent zone. Wait until the NS record and corresponding A record are removed from your parent zone. After the move, change the name server's A record in your zone data and add the name server's NS record to your zone data. Then use your registrar's interface to request that an NS record delegating the zone to the name server at its new address be added to the parent zone.

If you only have two authoritative name servers, consider adding another and using the previous solution. If you can't do that, arrange to have the name server answer on both its old and new addresses for a period of time (for example, by adding an IP address alias on the name server's network interface). Then change the name server's A record in your zone and in your parent zone through your registrar. (You may do this through the same form that you use to register a name server, or at least a similar form.) Once you see the new record in your parent zone, wait until one TTL has passed. Then remove the old address from your name server's configuration.

Discussion

The reason this is more complicated than moving a plain vanilla host is that a name server's address usually appears in two places: your own zone's data file and your parent zone. While you have direct control over your own zone, you must request changes to your parent zone through your registrar. And you can't be sure when the change to your parent zone will occur: it often takes a day or two for changes to take effect.

That's why removing the delegation to the name server that's moving ahead of time works well. It gives you the freedom to change the name server's address whenever you like. Then, after you've moved the name server, you can add it back at your leisure.

The reason this method doesn't work if you only have two name servers is that you never want to be left with only one authoritative name server for your zone. Consequently, you can't remove the delegation to a name server in advance of the move. You also shouldn't request the change of address through your registrar and try to synchronize the move with the change to your parent zone, since you'll inevitably end up with only one registered name server, at least for a little while.

See Also

Recipes 1.5 and 1.6 for information on the registration process, and Recipe 2.16 for the related process of changing data about a host that's not a name server.

6.7   Changing Your Zone's Name Servers

Problem

You want to change all of the registered name servers for your zone.

Solution

If you can, arrange to have the old name servers running and authoritative for your zone throughout the change. This still makes the process easier.

First, configure the new name servers as authoritative for your zone (or, if they're run by someone else, like your ISP, ask that they set them up). Once the new name servers are configured and answering authoritatively to queries in your zone, add NS records to your zone data for the new name servers and request that your registrar add those name servers to your zone's delegation information. When the delegation information has been updated in your parent zone, request that your registrar remove the delegation to the old name servers. Once that delegation information is gone from your parent zone, wait for one TTL on the delegation records to pass, then remove the NS records for the old name servers from the zone and, if you want, decommission the old name servers.

Discussion

Arranging to have both sets (old and new) of your name servers running simultaneously helps you make the required changes on your own schedule. It would be nearly impossible to coordinate the simultaneous decommissioning of the old name servers and commissioning of the new name servers with the changes to your zone's delegation information in your parent zone. With both sets running at once, you can ask your registrar to add the new ones, wait for the new delegation information to appear, then ask the registrar to delete the old ones.

When you establish the new authoritative name servers, you may initially want to configure them as slaves for your zone, loading from the primary master. If the primary master is among the name servers being decommissioned, you can later move the primary to one of the new name servers and reconfigure the other slaves to transfer from the new primary.

See Also

Recipes 1.5 and 1.6 for information on the registration process, and Recipe 6.6 for instructions on moving just one name server.

CHAPTER 7
Security

7.0 Introduction

Name server security is no great mystery. It's largely a matter of understanding the services a name server provides, then making sure it provides them only to authorized entities. Most name servers provide authoritative name service, recursive name service, and zone transfers, and some handle dynamic updates, too. Typically, you'll want to limit a name server to:

- Accepting recursive queries from the resolvers that are authorized to use it
- Accepting any nonrecursive queries in zones it's authoritative for
- Providing zone transfers only to authorized slaves
- Accepting dynamic updates only from authorized updaters

There are also a few operating system–level precautions you can take, such as running a name server in a *chroot()* "jail" and running it as a user other than root.

The trick, then, is identifying who's authorized to use the name server's services, and configuring the name server to enforce the necessary restrictions. This chapter helps you do both.

7.1 Concealing a Name Server's Version

Problem

Modern BIND name servers respond with their version to queries for TXT records attached to the pseudo-domain name *version.bind* in the CHAOSNET class. For example:

```
$ dig version.bind txt chaos

; <<>> DiG 9.2.1 <<>> version.bind txt chaos
;; global options:  printcmd
```

```
;; Got answer:
;; ->>HEADER<<- opcode: QUERY, status: NOERROR, id: 5096
;; flags: qr aa rd; QUERY: 1, ANSWER: 1, AUTHORITY: 0, ADDITIONAL: 0

;; QUESTION SECTION:
;version.bind.                    CH      TXT

;; ANSWER SECTION:
version.bind.           0        CH      TXT     "9.2.1"
```

You want to conceal the version a name server returns.

Solution

The simplest way to accomplish this is to use the *version options* substatement. The *version* substatement takes it as a string to return to *version.bind* queries as an argument. For example:

```
options {
    directory "/var/named";
    version "None of your business";
};
```

Some folks, however, don't want their name servers to return *anything*, not even a bogus answer, to unauthorized queriers. Others want authorized queriers to see the real version instead of a bogus one.

To set that up, create a CHAOSNET zone called *bind* and a *zone* statement for it in *named.conf*. Then use *allow-query* to restrict queries to the zone. Here's a sample *bind* zone data file:

```
$TTL 1d
@   CH   SOA    ns1.foo.example.   hostmaster.foo.example.   (
    2002052600 86400 3600 604800 3600 )
    CH   NS    ns1.foo.example.

version.bind.   CH   TXT   "BIND 9.2.1"
```

Notice that the records in the *bind* zone are all in the CHAOSNET class, as you would expect.

On a BIND 8 name server, the *zone* statement for the *bind* zone might look like this:

```
zone "bind" chaos {
    type master;
    file "db.bind";
    allow-query { localnets; };
};
```

On BIND 9, the configuration is a little more complicated. Even if you don't explicitly use views, BIND 9 creates zones in an implicit "default" view in the Internet class. So you can't just create a CHAOSNET zone in the default view, because the zone and the view have different classes: you need to create a new CHAOSNET view and define the *bind* zone in it. And, if you weren't using views before, you need to create an explicit Internet view for your other zones and move their *zone* statements into the view.

For example, if your BIND 9 name server's *named.conf* file looks like this now:

```
options {
    directory "/var/named";
};

zone "foo.example" {
    type master;
    file "db.foo.example";
};
```

You might change it to look like this:

```
options {
    directory "/var/named";
};

view internet in {

    zone "foo.example" {
        type master;
        file "db.foo.example";
    };
};

view chaosnet chaos {

    zone "bind" {
        type master;
        file "db.bind";
        allow-query { localnets; };
    };
};
```

Discussion

Camouflaging a name server's version is no substitute for running an up-to-date version of BIND or for configuring the name server securely. About the best you can hope for is that concealing a name server's version will prevent hackers from identifying it as an obvious, first-choice target if the version of BIND it's running has a vulnerability.

See Also

"BIND Version" in Chapter 11 of *DNS and BIND*.

7.2 Configuring a Name Server to Work with a Firewall (or Vice Versa)

Problem

You want to configure a name server to work through a firewall, or configure a firewall to work with a name server.

Solution

Configure your firewall to pass the UDP and TCP traffic that a BIND name server requires. This matrix shows you the traffic necessary for each purpose.

Purpose	Protocol	Source address	Source port	Destination address	Destination port
Queries from your name server	UDP or TCP	Your name server	> 1023	Any	53
Responses to your name server	UDP or TCP	Any	53	Your name server	> 1023
Queries from remote name servers	UDP or TCP	Any	> 1023	Your name server	53
Responses to remote name servers	UDP or TCP	Your name server	53	Any	> 1023

Refresh queries—the queries a slave name server sends to its master name server to see if a zone's serial number has increased—and NOTIFY messages are also sent from a high-numbered port (above 1023) to port 53.

Discussion

Normally, BIND name servers choose a source port to use for outbound queries when they start, which means you must allow DNS messages from any unprivileged port. However, you can configure a name server to use a particular source port for outbound queries with the *query-source options* substatement. (On BIND 8 name servers, *query-source* also controls the source port for NOTIFY messages and refresh queries.) For example, to instruct a name server to use port 1053 as the source port for all outbound queries, use:

```
options {
    directory "/var/named";
    query-source address * port 1053;
};
```

This may let you simplify the firewall rules somewhat, because you can limit outbound, UDP-based query traffic to a single source port. If the name server has multiple network interfaces, you can also use the *query-source* substatement to choose which

---

source address it uses in queries. For example, to tell a name server to use 192.168.0.1 as the source address in queries, use:

```
options {
    directory "/var/named";
    query-source address 192.168.0.1;
};
```

You can specify both the source address and source port, too:

```
options {
    directory "/var/named";
    query-source address 192.168.0.1 port 1053;
};
```

If you run a BIND 9 name server, use the *transfer-source* substatement in a *zone*, *view* or *options* statement to specify the source port used in refresh queries and forwarded dynamic updates. For example:

```
zone "foo.example" {
    type slave;
    masters { 192.168.0.1; };
    file "bak.foo.example";
    transfer-source * port 1053;
};
```

This tells the name server to use port 1053 as the source for all refresh queries and dynamic updates it forwards. The port specification doesn't apply to zone transfers, however, that use TCP; for TCP-based traffic, the source port is always chosen randomly. The address specification (here, "*") does apply to the source *address* of TCP zone transfer requests, though.

On BIND 8 name servers, *transfer-source* is only a *zone* substatement until BIND 8.2.2, when it's also supported as an *options* substatement. It only sets the source address used in zone transfers (that is, you can't specify a *port* argument):

```
options {
    directory "/var/named";
    transfer-source 192.168.0.2;
};
```

For NOTIFY messages, BIND 9.1.0 and later and BIND 8.3.2 and later name servers understand the *notify-source* substatement, which has the same argument syntax as *transfer-source* and can also be used as a *zone*, *view*, or *options* substatement.

Remember that queries can be TCP-based as well as UDP-based, so you must allow traffic from queriers to TCP port 53 as well as UDP port 53, and from your name server to TCP port 53.

See Also

"Configuring the IPv4 Transport" in Chapter 10 of *DNS and BIND*.

7.3 Setting Up a Hidden Primary Master Name Server

Problem

You want to run a primary master name server "hidden," so that other name servers don't query it.

Solution

Configure the slave name servers for your zones to use the primary master as their master name server, but don't list the primary master in the zones' NS records. For example, if *ns1.foo.example*, at 192.168.0.1, is the primary master name server for *foo.example*, you'd add *zone* statements like these to the slaves' *named.conf* files:

```
zone "foo.example" {
    type slave;
    masters { 192.168.0.1; };
    file "bak.foo.example";
};
```

But the NS records for *foo.example* wouldn't include *ns1.foo.example*:

```
foo.example.    IN    NS    ns2.foo.example.
foo.example.    IN    NS    ns.isp.net.
```

In addition, make sure the delegation information for *foo.example* does not include *ns1.foo.example*.

Discussion

"Hidden primary" configurations are often used to give the administrator of the primary master name server direct control over zone data without incurring any of the zone's query load. For example, a broadband Internet customer could run a local primary master name server on which to administer the zone, but leave his ISP's slaves to answer queries for data in the zone.

If you use Microsoft dynamic update clients, such as Windows 2000, be sure to list the real primary master name server in the MNAME field of the SOA records of dynamically updated zones. Microsoft dynamic update clients will send their updates to the name server designated in the MNAME field regardless of whether that name server also appears in the zone's NS records.

Clients with BIND-based update code will only send updates to name servers listed in a zone's NS records, so make sure your zones' slave name servers support update forwarding (that is, run BIND name servers from 9.1.0 on) and have update forwarding configured. See Recipe 3.11 for instructions on configuring update forwarding.

See Also

Recipe 3.11, for configuring update forwarding.

7.4   Setting Up a Stealth Slave Name Server

Problem

You want to set up a stealth slave name server, one that isn't queried by remote name servers.

Solution

Configure the name server as you would any other slave, but don't include it in the NS records for the zone (or zones) it's authoritative for.

Discussion

A stealth slave name server is a close cousin of a hidden primary master. Like a hidden primary, a stealth slave isn't included in the NS records for the zone it's authoritative for. Other than that, though, it has the same configuration as any other slave name server for that zone.

The function of a stealth slave name server may not be as obvious as that of a hidden primary. A hidden primary's benefit—making it possible to manage a zone without the burden of serving queries for the zone—doesn't apply to a stealth slave. So what's a stealth slave *for*?

Sometimes, you need another authoritative name server for a zone to serve some group of resolvers. Say you need a name server on a particular subnet, to serve the local resolvers. All of the subnet's resolvers live in the same zone, so they'll probably generate lots of queries for domain names in that zone. Shouldn't their local name server be authoritative for the zone?

But what if you already have as many NS records for the zone as you can fit in a UDP-based DNS message (usually 10 or 11)? Or what if you don't want remote name servers to query the new slave, because the subnet it's on isn't well-connected to the rest of the network? Just don't list it in the zone's NS records: remote name servers won't follow delegation to it, but you can configure local resolvers to query it directly.

Since the slave isn't in the list of NS records for the zone, the zone's other authoritative name servers won't send it NOTIFY messages by default. You'll have to configure the stealth slave's master name server to send it NOTIFY messages; for instructions, see Recipe 3.12.

See Also

Recipe 3.12 for configuring the stealth slave's master name server to send NOTIFY messages to the stealth slave.

7.5 Configuring an Authoritative-Only Name Server

Problem

You want to configure an "authoritative-only" or nonrecursive name server.

Solution

Disable recursion with the *recursion options* substatement:

```
options {
    directory "/var/named";
    recursion no;
};
```

If the name server isn't already configured as authoritative for one or more zones, add *zone* statements to *named.conf*, too.

Discussion

Since "authoritative-only" isn't a standard term (nor is "nonrecursive," really), a few words of explanation are in order. A nonrecursive or authoritative-only name server is one that only answers nonrecursive queries from remote name servers. It can't directly serve resolvers, since all resolvers send recursive queries by default, but you can delegate zones to it, and it's nearly invulnerable to spoofing attacks, since it normally doesn't send queries. It's also more resistant to denial of service attacks, since it doesn't process resource-intensive recursive queries.

For completeness, you may also want to disable glue fetching on BIND 8 name servers:

```
options {
    directory "/var/named";
    recursion no;
    fetch-glue no;
};
```

This step prevents the name server from sending queries to look up A records for name servers that appear in NS records. That, together with disabling recursion, makes the name server completely passive. It may prevent NOTIFY from working correctly, though, since the name server won't look up the addresses of name servers outside of the zones it's authoritative for. In that case, use Recipe 3.13 to configure the name server to send NOTIFY messages to the slaves explicitly.

Remember to limit concurrent zone transfers (Recipe 5.16) and accept only authorized zone transfer requests (Recipe 7.10) if the name server acts as a master.

See Also

Recipe 3.13, for explicit NOTIFY configuration; Recipe 5.16, to limit concurrent zone transfers; and Recipe 7.10, for adding zone transfer restrictions.

7.6   Configuring a Caching-Only Name Server

Problem

You want to configure a caching-only name server.

Solution

Configure the name server with a root hints file (or, if you run BIND 9, use the built-in root hints) and restrict the queries it handles to the addresses of authorized resolvers using the *allow-query options* substatement. For example:

```
acl internal { 192.168.0/24; };

options {
    directory "/var/named";
    allow-query { internal; };
};

// The root hints are compiled into a BIND 9 name server, so this zone
// statement is optional on those name servers

zone "." {
    type hint;
    file "db.cache";
};
```

Discussion

You may want to set up a caching-only name server as authoritative for some internal zones, so that you can ensure that data in those zones is reliable. In this configuration, the name server will ignore records from your internal zones in answers from remote name servers, making it hard for a hacker to spoof data in those zones.

Since a caching-only name server's main function is to query other name servers and cache the results, follow the instructions in Recipe 7.14 to protect against spoofing.

See Also

Recipe 7.14 for instructions on protecting a name server from spoofing.

7.7   Running a Name Server in a chroot( ) Jail

Problem

You want to run a name server in a *chroot( )* jail, so that a hacker successfully breaking in through the *named* process has limited access to the host's filesystem.

Solution

Set up an environment for the name server to *chroot( )* into, then use *named*'s *–t* command-line option to specify the name of the directory to *chroot( )* to.

A BIND 9 *chroot( )* environment, on most Unix systems, should include:

- A working directory for the name server (which can be the *chroot( )* directory itself)
- An *etc* subdirectory, which includes *named.conf* and the *localtime* file, copied from */etc/localtime*
- A *var/run* subdirectory for the name server's PID file
- A *dev* subdirectory, which may need to include the *log*, *random*, and *zero* devices

On my FreeBSD system, here's how I set up the *chroot( )* environment:

```
# mkdir /etc/namedb
# cd /etc/namedb
# mkdir -p dev etc/namedb var/run etc/namedb is the working directory
# cp /etc/localtime etc
# mknod dev/random c 2 3
# mknod dev/zero c 2 12
# vi etc/named.conf
```

To create the *log* device, I added the command-line option *–a /etc/namedb/dev/log* to the startup of the *syslog* daemon. This tells *syslogd* to create an extra *log* device with the specified path (in the *chroot( )* environment) and listen on it for logged messages.

Piece of cake!

Once you've set up the *chroot( )* environment, start *named* with the *–t* command-line option, specifying the directory to *chroot( )* to as the option's argument. The first time you do it, check *named*'s *syslog* output for any startup errors caused by missing files or directories. Once *named* starts cleanly in the *chroot( )* environment, add the *–t* option to your system's startup scripts.

Discussion

When running a name server in a *chroot()* environment, be sure to run as a non-root user, too. On many operating systems, a hacker gaining access to a process as root can break out of a *chroot()* jail. See Recipe 7.8 for instructions on running *named* as a non-root user.

BIND 8 name servers require a considerably more complicated *chroot()* environment, including a *passwd* file, shared libraries (unless you build BIND statically linked), and various device files, which is a good reason to recommend using BIND 9 in a *chroot()d* setup. If you insist on running a BIND 8 name server *chroot()ed*, see "Running BIND with Least Privilege" in Chapter 11 of *DNS and BIND* for instructions.

You can simplify the *chroot()* environment slightly by using the *pid-file options* substatement to tell *named* to create the PID file with a different pathname. For example, to create the PID file in the name server's working directory, use:

```
options {
    directory "/var/named";
    pid-file "named.pid";
};
```

In fact, unless you use dynamically updated zones with DNSSEC, you can do without *dev/random* in the *chroot()* environment, too. But then you'll have to put up with *named* logging an error each time it starts.

See Also

Recipe 1.20 for editing startup scripts, Recipe 7.8 for running BIND as a user other than root, and "Running BIND with Least Privilege" in Chapter 11 of *DNS and BIND*.

7.8 Running the Name Server as a User Other than Root

Problem

You want to run a name server as a user other than root, so a hacker successfully breaking in through the *named* process doesn't have access to the host as root.

Solution

Add a *passwd* file entry for a new user; the only function of this file is to run the name server. Call this user something descriptive, such as *bind* or *named*. A *passwd* entry for a *bind* user might look like this:

```
bind:*:53:53:BIND name server:/:/bin/nologin
```

Optionally, add a *group* file entry for a new group, which this new user and any other users who are authorized to edit zone data file will belong to.

Adjust the ownership and permission of files and directories to make sure that this user (and group, if you created one) can:

- Read, write and execute (search) *named*'s working directory
- Read and write all zone data files
- Write to the */var/run* directory (unless you've used the *pid-file options* substatement to change the PID file's path)

Once you've modified the environment as needed, start *named* with the *–u* command-line option, specifying as the option's argument the name or user ID of the user to run as. The first time you do it, check *named*'s *syslog* output for any startup errors caused by permission problems. Once *named* starts cleanly, add the *–u* option to your system's startup scripts.

Discussion

Note that, as long as *named* is configured to listen on port 53, the default port, it must be *started* by root, since port 53 is a privileged port. The *–u* option simply tells it to give up root privilege as soon as it's done what it needs to do as root.

As Recipe 7.7 says, name servers that run in a *chroot()* environment normally run as a non-root user, too, to prevent hackers from escaping the *chroot()* jail.

BIND 8 name servers also support a *–g* command-line option to set the name server's group ID. If *–g* isn't specified, the name server changes group to the primary group of the user specified in the *–u* option. BIND 9 name servers don't support *–g*, and always change group to the primary group of the user named in *–u*.

On a BIND 8 name server, you may also need to change the group membership and permissions of the *ndc* Unix domain socket in order to allow users in the *bind* group to write to it.

See Also

Recipe 1.20 for editing startup scripts, Recipe 7.7 for running a name server in a *chroot()* environment, and "Running BIND with Least Privilege" in Chapter 11 of *DNS and BIND*.

7.9   Defining a TSIG Key

Problem

You want to define a TSIG key for use in authenticating remote name servers and dynamic updaters.

Solution

Add a *key* statement to the name server's *named.conf* file defining the new TSIG key. For example:

```
key dhcp-server.foo.example {
    algorithm hmac-md5;
    secret "OqprPEyzGITPOT7FcES7Wg==";
};
```

The first argument is the name of the key—in this case, *dhcp-server.foo.example*. The key is often named after one or both of the hosts that use it. The algorithm substatement specifies the cryptographic algorithm the key is used with; for TSIG, it is always *hmac-md5*. The secret is the base 64 encoding of the binary TSIG key.

You can generate the key with *dnssec-keygen* or *dnskeygen*, programs included in the BIND 9 and BIND 8 distributions, respectively. To generate the key above, I used the command:

```
$ dnssec-keygen –a HMAC-MD5 –b 128 -n HOST dhcp-server.foo.example
Kdhcp-server.foo.example.+157+19185
```

The argument to the *–a* ("algorithm") option specified the cryptographic algorithm as HMAC-MD5, while the argument to *–b* ("bit length") specified the length of the key to generate, in bits. The *–n* ("nametype") option specified this key as a host key, and the only non-option argument specified the name of the key. The program then printed a string to standard output (*Kdhcp-server.foo.example.+157+19185*) that identified the name of a file it wrote the key to. (The name of the file is actually that string with ".key" appended.) The file contained:

```
dhcp-server.foo.example. IN KEY 512 3 157 OqprPEyzGITPOT7FcES7Wg==
```

The last field is the base 64 encoding of the random, 128-bit key it generated.

The *key* statement should be identical—including both the name of the key and the secret—in the *named.conf* file of both name servers (or the name server and updater) that will use it.

Discussion

Defining a TSIG key doesn't do anything useful by itself; it just makes the key available for the name server to use. The key still needs to be applied to some security mechanism, as in an *allow-transfer* substatement (Recipe 7.10).

It's safest to define unique TSIG keys for use between any two name servers, so that the compromise of one TSIG key doesn't cause a broader security failure.

The maximum length of a TSIG key is 512 bits. Longer keys are harder to break, but 128 bits should be ample for all but the most paranoid administrators.

dnskeygen takes very similar arguments to *dnssec-keygen*; check the manual page for details. And if you can't figure out how to use *dnskeygen*, you can always build *dnssec-keygen* and use it to generate TSIG keys for your BIND 8 name server.

TSIG requires time synchronization between the name servers or the name server and updater that will use it. Getting the clocks within about five minutes of each other is all that's necessary, though. You can do that with any respectable time synchronization service, from *rdate* to NTP.

See Also

Recipe 3.10, for securing dynamic updates with TSIG, and Recipe 7.10, for securing zone transfers using TSIG.

7.10 Securing Zone Transfers

Problem

You want to secure zone transfers from a name server.

Solution

Use the *allow-transfer* substatement to specify the addresses of slave name servers allowed to transfer zones. Or, even better, define a TSIG key on the master and slave name servers (see Recipe 7.9), and specify the TSIG key in the *allow-transfer* substatement.

allow-transfer can be used as either an *options* substatement or as a *zone* substatement. As a *zone* substatement, *allow-transfer* applies only to transfers of that zone, and overrides any *allow-transfer options* substatement for transfers of that zone.

For example, to restrict transfers of the zone *foo.example* to the slave name server at 192.168.0.2, you might use this *zone* statement:

```
zone "foo.example" {
    type master;
    file "db.foo.example";
    allow-transfer { 192.168.0.2; };
};
```

To restrict transfers of all authoritative zones to slave name servers signing their requests with the TSIG key *ns1-ns2.foo.example*, you might use the following *options* statement:

```
options {
    directory "/var/named";
    allow-transfer { key ns1-ns2.foo.example; };
};
```

The keyword *key* is necessary to distinguish the name of the TSIG key from a named ACL.

Obviously, the slave doesn't need any special configuration to initiate its zone transfers from its own address, but it does require configuration to tell it to sign requests with a particular TSIG key. To tell a slave to sign all zone transfer requests to the name server at 192.168.0.1 with the key *ns1-ns2.foo.example*, you could add the following server statement to *named.conf*:

```
server 192.168.0.1 {
    keys ns1-ns2.foo.example;
};
```

Discussion

For readability's sake, consider defining ACLs with descriptive names even when you're only using IP addresses in your *allow-transfer* substatements. For example, you could rewrite the *zone* statement above like so:

```
acl ns2.foo.example { 192.168.0.2; };

zone "foo.example" {
    type master;
    file "db.foo.example";
    allow-transfer { ns2.foo.example; };
};
```

Isn't that better?

You can mix IP addresses and TSIG keys in an *allow-transfer* substatement, too, in which case the individual elements or logically OR'd together.

Restricting zone transfers to a slave name server by both a TSIG key and the slave's address is more difficult than you might imagine. First, define an ACL that matches all IP addresses *except* the address of the slave:

```
acl not-ns2.foo.example { !192.168.0.2; any; };
```

Use the negation of this ACL as the first term of the argument to *allow-transfer*, and the TSIG key as the second:

```
options {
    directory "/var/named";
    allow-transfer { !not-ns2.foo.example; key ns1-ns2.foo.example; };
};
```

The negation operator in the first term tells the name server to deny zone transfers from addresses that match the negated ACL, *not-ns2.foo.example*, and the negated ACL matches every address but that of the slave. In other words, the first term denies all addresses but the address of the slave. The next term guarantees that only requests from the slave that are signed with the specified TSIG key are permitted; any other requests from the address of the slave are implicitly denied.

Finally, remember that a BIND name server's default is to allow transfers of any zone, so you'll need to deny all transfers on slave name servers that don't serve any other slaves with:

```
allow-transfer { none; };
```

See Also

Recipe 7.9 for instructions on defining TSIG keys and "Preventing Unauthorized Zone Transfers" in Chapter 11 of *DNS and BIND*.

7.11 Restricting the Queries a Name Server Answers

Problem

You want to restrict the queries a name server answers.

Solution

Use the *allow-query* substatement to restrict the queries to which the name server responds. *allow-query* can be used as either an *options* substatement or a *zone* substatement. As an *options* substatement, it determines which addresses the name server will reply to for queries in any zone. Used as a *zone* substatement, *allow-query* controls which queriers can look up records in that zone, and overrides any eponymous *options* substatement.

This *allow-query* substatement allows only queriers (resolvers and name servers) on local networks to look up arbitrary domain names:

```
options {
    directory "/var/named";
    allow-query { localnets; };
};
```

The *localnets* ACL is predefined by BIND as all of the networks to which the host that runs the name server is directly connected.

In the same *named.conf* file, this *allow-query* substatement allows anyone to look up domain names in the *bar.example* zone:

```
zone "bar.example" {
    type slave;
    masters { 10.0.0.1; };
    file "bak.bar.example";
    allow-query { any; };
};
```

This particular combination of *allow-query* substatements is useful on name servers that serve some group of local resolvers that you can identify by IP address, but also have one or more zones delegated to them.

You can also control which addresses are allowed to send recursive queries with the *allow-recursion options* substatement, supported in BIND 8.2.1 and later. Only queriers in the specified address match list will have their queries processed recursively; all other queries and treated as nonrecursive. For example:

```
options {
    directory "/var/named";
    allow-recursion { localnets; };
};
```

Discussion

If you're faced with the choice of using multiple *allow-query* substatements or a single *allow-recursion* substatement to protect a name server from unauthorized queries, you should be aware of an important corner case: name servers authoritative for a zone that contains delegation may receive legitimate queries from remote name servers for data in subzones. The combination of *allow-query options* and *zone* substatements described earlier won't permit these queries, since the queries are received from nonlocal addresses for data outside of the name server's authoritative zones. *allow-recursion* works fine, though; you can permit recursive queries only from local networks and allow nonrecursive queries from anywhere.

Though you can specify TSIG keys with the *allow-query* substatement, there's usually not much point in doing so, since resolvers don't sign queries. Other name servers can, though.

See Also

"Restricting Queries" in Chapter 11 of *DNS and BIND*.

7.12 Preventing a Name Server from Querying a Particular Remote Name Server

Problem

You want to keep a name server from querying a particular remote name server.

Solution

Add a *server* statement to the name server's *named.conf* file, specifying the remote name server's IP address, with a *bogus* substatement telling the name server not to query it. For example:

```
server 192.168.0.255 {
    bogus yes;
};
```

Discussion

This feature isn't used much on production name servers, perhaps because there aren't many remote name servers that are known to be under the influence of evil organizations bent on world domination, à la SMERSH or SPECTRE. But it can come in handy if you know that a particular name server is misbehaving.

If you do add a *server* statement to keep a name server from speaking to a remote name server, remember to check back periodically to see if the remote name server is still suffering from whatever dyspepsia is causing it to belch forth unpleasantness.

See Also

"Avoiding a Bogus Name Server" in Chapter 10 of *DNS and BIND*.

7.13 Preventing a Name Server from Responding to DNS Traffic from Certain Networks

Problem

You want to prevent a name server from responding to any DNS traffic—queries, NOTIFY messages, dynamic updates—from certain networks.

Solution

List the networks in the *blackhole options* substatement. Any traffic the name server receives from addresses on these networks will be ignored. For example, this *blackhole* substatement tells the name server not to respond to queries from RFC 1918 address space:

```
options {
    directory "/var/named";
    blackhole {
        10/8; 172.16/12; 192.168/16;
    };
};
```

You might want to configure an external name server like this, to prevent it from wasting time replying to queries from private address space. Of course, this solution assumes that you don't use these networks internally.

Discussion

The difference between *blackhole* and *allow-query* is that a name server replies to a querier blocked by *allow-query* with a message indicating that its query was refused, while a name server doesn't respond at all to a querier in a list of blackholed networks.

There's a surprisingly long list of networks that name servers shouldn't respond to traffic from, because they correspond to experimental, multicast, or private address space. The excellent "Secure BIND Template," maintained by Rob Thomas, contains a *blackhole* substatement that includes a list of these networks.

If you go to the trouble of setting up such a complete *blackhole* substatement for your name servers, though, you may also want to consider configuring your border router to drop all traffic from those networks. This will protect all of your network services, not just DNS.

See Also

"Avoiding a Bogus Name Server" in Chapter 10 of *DNS and BIND*; and "The Secure BIND Template," which you can find at *http://www.cymru.com/~robt/Docs/Articles/secure-bind-template.html*.

7.14   Protecting a Name Server from Spoofing

Problem

You want to protect a name server from spoofing attacks.

Solution

On a BIND 8.2 or later name server, set the *use-id-pool options* substatement to *yes*. This tells the name server to use better, optional randomization routines to choose message IDs for the header of DNS queries. This makes the message IDs harder to guess, and, therefore, it is more difficult to spoof a response to those queries. (On a BIND 9 name server, you don't need *use-id-pool* since the better randomization routines are now standard.)

Also, use the *allow-recursion options* substatement, as described in Recipe 7.11, to restrict which networks the name server will accept recursive queries from. If it doesn't accept recursive queries from arbitrary addresses on the Internet, hackers will find it harder to induce the name server to query name servers under their control and thereby poison its cache.

Finally, you might use the technique introduced in Recipe 7.6, configuring the name server as authoritative for important internal zones. The name server will ignore records from your internal zones in answers from remote name servers, making it hard for a hacker to spoof data in those zones.

Discussion

If the name server doesn't serve any recursive queriers, of course, configure it as authoritative-only name server, as described in Recipe 7.5.

See Also

Recipe 7.6 for loading internal zones and Recipe 7.11 for use of the *allow-recursion* substatement, or Recipe 7.5 for configuring an authoritative-only name server.

CHAPTER 8

Interoperability and Upgrading

8.0   Introduction

Not all name servers run BIND. And, much as it may disappoint the authors of the various RFCs that standardize the DNS protocol, some of these non-catholic name servers don't interoperate with BIND name servers. With a little administrative arm-twisting, however, you can usually coax BIND and the alien name servers into a DNS détente. Recipes 8.3 through 8.5 cover this kind of diplomacy.

If you're a conscientious administrator, you'll upgrade your name servers when new versions are released, to close vulnerabilities and take advantage of new features. If you're making a big jump, from BIND 4 or BIND 8 to a newer release, Recipes 8.1 and 8.2 give helpful hints.

Finally, newer Windows operating systems use DNS for much more than mundane web browsing. Windows 2000 and XP computers use dynamic update to register their name-to-address and address-to-name mappings, and Domain Controllers use updates to add SRV records advertising the services they offer. While Microsoft made it easiest to serve these clients with the Microsoft DNS Server, BIND name servers are flexible enough to accommodate them, too. See Recipes 8.7 and 8.8 for details.

8.1   Upgrading from BIND 4 to BIND 8 or 9

Problem

You want to upgrade a name server from BIND 4 to BIND 8 or 9.

Solution

Convert the name server's *named.boot* file into an equivalent *named.conf* file using *named-bootconf.sh* or manually, if you prefer. You can find *named-bootconf.sh* in

BIND 9's *contrib/named-bootconf* directory, or in BIND 8's *bin/named-bootconf* directory. *named-bootconf* reads a file in *named.boot* format from standard input and writes a functionally equivalent *named.conf* file to standard output. So, for example, you could run it like this:

```
$ named-bootconf.sh < /etc/named.boot > named.conf
```

If you're upgrading to a version of BIND more recent than BIND 8.2, you'll also need to add a *$TTL* control statement to each of your zone data files. See Recipe 2.1 for an explanation of the *$TTL* control statement.

BIND 8 and 9 both have stricter rules governing the contents of a zone than BIND 4. For example, BIND 4 allowed you to attach multiple CNAME records to a single domain name; BIND 8 and 9 don't, by default. BIND 4 allowed you to attach a CNAME record and other record types to a single domain name; BIND 8 and 9 don't. It's a good idea to either use BIND 9's *named-checkzone* program (Recipe 5.2) to check the zone before loading it or examine the upgraded name server's *syslog* output closely after starting it.

BIND 4 name servers also send all UDP traffic from port 53, whereas newer name servers use a random source port. After upgrading, you may need to adjust firewall rules or configure the name server to use port 53 as its source port (Recipe 7.2).

Discussion

Arguably more important than any of this is that the newest BIND 8 and 9 name servers fix many bugs and vulnerabilities, and support *many* new security features. Take a look at Chapter 7 to get an idea of how you can secure a brand-spanking new name server.

If you still have BIND 4 name servers running as slaves to this name server, see Recipe 8.3 for instructions on how to accommodate the older name servers.

See Also

Recipe 2.1 for coverage of the *$TTL* control statement, Recipe 5.2 for how to drive *named-checkzone*, and Recipe 7.2 for the getting a BIND name server to work with a firewall.

8.2 Upgrading from BIND 8 to BIND 9

Problem

You want to upgrade a name server from BIND 8 to BIND 9.

Solution

The good news is that BIND 9's configuration file format is the same as BIND 8's, so you won't need to convert your old *named.conf* file. However, BIND 9 name servers don't support some configuration options that BIND 8 name servers support. For a list, see the file *doc/misc/options* in the BIND 9 distribution. Options marked as "obsolete" or "not [yet] implemented" aren't supported. In most cases, you either won't need the old option or can make do with functionality provided by a newer option.

One major change in the configuration file is the *controls* statement. BIND 8 name servers support both *inet* and *unix* control channels (see Recipe 3.1). BIND 9, however, only supports a new type of *inet* control channel, so you'll probably need to modify the name server's *controls* statement and create an *rndc.conf* file, per Recipe 3.2.

The zone data file format is also the same in BIND 8 and BIND 9. However, if you're upgrading from a version of BIND older than 8.2 to BIND 9, you'll need to add *$TTL* control statements to your zone data files, as described in Recipe 8.1.

There are aspects of the name server's operation that change in BIND 9. For example, BIND 8 name servers will start even if there are (minor) syntax errors in the *named.conf* file. A BIND 9 name server won't. This forces you to fix any syntax errors before the name server will start, which is probably a good thing.

BIND 8 name servers will also load zone data files even if they contain (minor) errors. A BIND 9 name server won't. Again, this forces you to fix any errors in the data file before the name server will respond to any queries in the zone.

BIND 9 uses different logging categories than BIND 8 did, so if the name server's *named.conf* file includes a *logging* statement, you may need to modify it for use with BIND 9. For example, BIND 8 name servers log all messages not assigned to a category to the *default* category, whereas BIND 9 name servers log such messages to the *general* category. See "Category Details" in Chapter 7 of *DNS and BIND* for a list of all BIND 9 categories and how they correspond to BIND 8's categories.

Finally, BIND 9 name servers don't check whether domain names contain "valid" characters, so the *check-names* substatement doesn't work.

Discussion

Although it may not affect the name server you're upgrading, the default format BIND 9 uses for sending zone transfers is the many-answers format. BIND 8 name servers understand many-answers zone transfers, though they send one-answers zone transfers by default. If you have older slave name servers that don't speak many-answers, see Recipes 8.3 and 8.4 for instructions on configuring a BIND 9 name server to speak their language.

In a BIND 8 name server's *named.conf* file, you could add a *zone* statement of a non-IN class anywhere. In BIND 9, however, you must add non-IN *zone* statements to a non-IN view. That means using views and moving *all zone* statements into *view* statements, whether or not you have any other use for views. Recipe 7.1 shows an example of this.

For a more complete reckoning of the changes between BIND 8 and BIND 9 name servers, see the file *doc/misc/migration* in the BIND 9 distribution.

See Also

Recipes 3.1 and 3.2 for the differences in the syntax of the *controls* statement in BIND 8 and 9, Recipes 8.3 and 8.4 for instructions on serving old-style, one-answer zone transfers to BIND 4 name servers, Recipe 7.1 for an example of setting up a non-IN class view, and the "Category Details" section of Chapter 7 of *DNS and BIND* for lists of categories supported by BIND 8 and BIND 9 name servers.

8.3   Configuring a Name Server to Accommodate a Slave Running BIND 4

Problem

You need to configure a name server to accommodate a BIND 4 slave.

Solution

On a BIND 9 name server, you may need to configure the name server to send old-style, one-answer zone transfers to the slave. Add a *server* statement specifying the slave's address, and use the *transfer-format* substatement to set the transfer format to *one-answer*:

```
server 192.168.0.2 {
    transfer-format one-answer;
};
```

BIND 8 name servers send one-answer zone transfers by default, so there's no need to add a *server* statement especially for a BIND 4 slave—unless you've changed the default in a *transfer-format options* substatement.

You'll also need to avoid adding resource records to zones that were introduced after the version of BIND that the slave runs. In particular, watch out for SRV records, introduced in BIND 4.9.5.

Discussion

Since the ISC has deprecated the use of any version of BIND 4, you should also prod the administrator of the BIND 4 slave to upgrade.

See Also

"More efficient zone transfers" in Chapter 10 of *DNS and BIND*, and the ISC's BIND pages, at *http://www.isc.org/products/BIND/*, for recommended versions of BIND.

8.4   Configuring a BIND Name Server to Accommodate a Slave Running the Microsoft DNS Server

Problem

You need to configure a BIND name server to accommodate a slave running the Microsoft DNS Server.

Solution

Although the version of the Microsoft DNS Server that shipped with Windows 2000 Server nominally supports many-answers zone transfers, some versions have trouble with DNS messages larger than 16K—exactly the kind a many-answers zone transfer might include. If you're running a BIND 9 name server, which sends many-answers zone transfers by default, you may need to add a *server* statement telling the name server to send one-answer zone transfers to the Microsoft DNS Server. For example:

```
server 10.0.0.1 {
    transfer-format one-answer;
};
```

Also, the Microsoft DNS Server doesn't handle some record types, including A6, DNAME, and all DNSSEC-related records (KEY, SIG and NXT), so make sure you don't add those to the zone.

Discussion

Unfortunately, transfers to the Microsoft DNS Server fail nearly silently if the zone contains these record types, making it difficult for the administrator to diagnose.

See Also

Section 3.2 of the file *doc/misc/migration* in the BIND 9 distribution.

8.5   Configuring a BIND Name Server as a Slave to a Microsoft DNS Server

Problem

You want to configure a BIND name server as a slave to a Microsoft DNS Server.

Solution

Configure the BIND name server as a slave for the zones you want to load from the Microsoft DNS Server, using the Microsoft DNS Server's address in the zones' *masters* substatements.

On the Microsoft DNS Server, make sure the name server doesn't include WINS or WINS-R records in zone transfers to your BIND slave. (You're adding a WINS record when you configure a Microsoft DNS Server to look up names using a WINS server if it can't find them in a zone, and a WINS-R record when you configure the name server to use a NETBIOS query to help with reverse mapping.) These records are included in zone transfers unless you check the *Do not replicate this record* checkbox on the *WINS* tab of the zone's *Properties* window in the DNS Console (for Windows 2000) or the *Settings only affect local server* checkbox on the *WINS Lookup* tab of the zone's *Properties* window in DNS Manager (for Windows NT 4.0).

Discussion

Remember to ask the administrator of the zone to add an NS record for the name server, assuming you want remote name servers to query it. If you don't want the name server listed in an NS record, you can still ask the administrator to configure his Microsoft DNS Server to send your name server NOTIFY messages for the slave zones.

See Also

"Interoperability and Version Problems" in Chapter 14 of *DNS and BIND*, and "Interoperability Problems" in Chapter 13 of *DNS on Windows 2000*.

8.6   Preventing Windows Computers from Trying to Update Your Zones

Problem

You want to prevent computers running Windows 2000 and XP from trying to dynamically update your zones.

Solution

On the Windows computer, go to *Start → Settings → Network and Dial-up Connections*. For each network interface, right-click on the name of the interface and choose *Properties*. In the *Properties* window, double-click on *Internet Protocol (TCP/IP)*. In the *Internet Protocol (TCP/IP) Properties* window, click on *Advanced...*. Finally, in the *Advanced TCP/IP Settings* window, click on the *DNS* tab. Uncheck *Register this connection's addresses in DNS* and click *OK*.

If you prefer to monkey around with the Registry, you can accomplish the same thing for all interfaces by adding a *REG_DWORD* value called *DisableDynamicUpdate*, with a value of 1, to the Registry key *HKEY_LOCAL_MACHINE\System\CurrentControlSet\ Services\Tcpip\Parameters\ Interfaces*.

Discussion

Computers running Windows 2000 and XP, by default, try to register their name-to-address and address-to-name mappings using dynamic update. (Well, that's not completely true: DHCP clients register their name-to-address mappings, but their DHCP servers normally add the address-to-name mappings.) Of course, unless you expressly allow such updates by adding an *allow-update* substatement to your *zone* statements, your name server will deny those updates. However, you may get sick of seeing errors like these in *syslog*:

```
Jun  5 13:56:07 ns1 named[50684]: error: client 192.168.0.254#3181: update foo.
example/IN' denied
```

These messages are logged to the *security* category, and you certainly don't want to discard all security-related messages, so it's important to know how to stop the updates at their source.

In BIND 9.3.0, those messages are in the *update-security* category, so you can send those messages to the *null* channel without missing more important security-relevant messages.

See Also

Recipe 8.7, in case you want to do something productive with those dynamic updates.

8.7 Handling Windows Registration with a BIND Name Server

Problem

You want to allow your computers running Windows 2000 and XP to register using dynamic update.

Solution

There are several techniques for dealing with Windows computers' desire to register their name-to-address and address-to-name mappings, but one of the most popular is to create a special subzone just for the computers to register in. If your main forward-mapping zone is *corp.example*, you might create a *dyn.corp.example subzone* for the Windows computers to live in. The name servers for *dyn.corp.example* don't need to be different from the name servers that serve *corp.example*; what's important is that the zones are separate. This lets you allow dynamic updates to one while keeping the other static.

The delegation for *dyn.corp.example* in the *corp.example* zone might look like this:

```
dyn.corp.example.    IN    NS    ns1.corp.example.
dyn.corp.example.    IN    NS    ns2.corp.example.
```

dyn.corp.example could begin life as a minimal zone, with just an SOA record and NS records:

```
$TTL 1d
@    IN    SOA    ns1.corp.example.    hostmaster.corp.example.    (
     2002061900
     1h
     15m
     30d
     1h )
     IN    NS    ns1.corp.example.
     IN    NS    ns2.corp.example.
```

Over time, of course, computers running Windows will register themselves and "fill out" the contents of the zone.

The name servers for *dyn.corp.example* must allow dynamic updates from the addresses of any Windows computers that might register. For example:

```
acl dhcp-clients { 192.168.0.128/25; };
acl static-clients { 192.168.0.64/26; };
```

```
zone "dyn.corp.example" {
    type master;
    file "db.dyn.corp.example";
    allow-update { dhcp-clients; static-clients; };
};
```

Finally, the Windows computers must be configured with *dyn.corp.example* as their *primary DNS suffix*, Microsoft's term for a local domain name. Go to *My Computer* → *Properties* → *Network Identification* → *Properties* → *More…* Enter *dyn.corp.example* in the field labeled *Primary DNS Suffix*. If the local domain name is different from the name of the Windows domain the computer is part of, uncheck *Change primary DNS Suffix if domain Membership Changes* checkbox before setting it.

Discussion

All this work is necessary because allowing dynamic updates to your main forward-mapping zone from just any old computer running Windows 2000 or XP is a bad idea. One of those users could easily download a copy of BIND, precompiled for Windows computers, and use *nsupdate* to modify the zone. And with unsigned dynamic updates—the only kind that currently work between Windows computers and BIND name servers—there are no restrictions to what he could change in the zone. By cordoning off the Windows computers in their own zone, they can only hurt each other.

If you're not comfortable with the idea of allowing dynamic updates to a subzone from all of your Windows machines, you might consider using DHCP to assign their addresses—even the addresses of statically addressed hosts—and configuring the DHCP server to assume responsibility for updating its clients' forward- and reverse-mapping information. Most modern DHCP servers support this. With this configuration, you can allow dynamic updates only from the address of your DHCP server. You can also restrict dynamic updates to your reverse-mapping zones to just your DHCP server, which helps minimize the threat to those zones. See Recipe 8.9 for instructions on configuring one DHCP server, the ISC's, to update a forward- and reverse-mapping zone.

See Also

"DNS and Windows 2000" in Chapter 16 of *DNS and BIND*; and "The Ties That BIND" in the March, 2001, issue of Linux Magazine, at *http://www.linux-mag.com/2001-03/bind_01.html*.

8.8 Handling Active Directory with a Name Server

Problem

You want to allow your Active Directory Domain Controllers to register their SRV records using dynamic update.

Solution

As with Recipe 8.7, there are a number of different solutions to this problem, but this is probably the most popular. If your Windows domain has the same name as an existing zone in DNS, create subzones with the names:

- _msdcs.name-of-Windows-2000-domain
- _sites.name-of-Windows-2000-domain
- _tcp.name-of-Windows-2000-domain
- _udp.name-of-Windows-2000-domain

For example, if both the name of your Windows domain and the domain name of your main forward-mapping zone were *corp.example*, you would create zones called *_msdcs.corp.example*, *_sites.corp.example*, *_tcp.corp.example*, and *_udp.corp.example*. You don't need separate name servers for these zones; they can be the same as the *corp.example* name servers:

```
_msdcs.corp.example.    IN    NS    ns1.corp.example.
_msdcs.corp.example.    IN    NS    ns2.corp.example.

_sites.corp.example.    IN    NS    ns1.corp.example.
_sites.corp.example.    IN    NS    ns2.corp.example.

_tcp.corp.example.      IN    NS    ns1.corp.example.
_tcp.corp.example.      IN    NS    ns2.corp.example.

_udp.corp.example.      IN    NS    ns1.corp.example.
_udp.corp.example.      IN    NS    ns2.corp.example.
```

Like the special subzone for Windows hosts to register in, these zones can start as minimal zones:

```
$TTL 1d
@    IN    SOA    ns1.corp.example.    hostmaster.corp.example.    (
     2002061900
     1h
     15m
     30d
     1h )
     IN    NS    ns1.corp.example.
     IN    NS    ns2.corp.example.
```

However, we only need to permit dynamic updates to these zones that come from our Domain Controllers:

```
acl domain-controllers { 192.168.0.100; 192.168.0.200; };

zone "_msdcs.corp.example" {
    type master;
    file "db._msdcs.corp.example";
    allow-update { domain-controllers; };
};

zone "_sites.corp.example" {
    type master;
    file "db._sites.corp.example";
    allow-update { domain-controllers; };
};

zone "_tcp.corp.example" {
    type master;
    file "db._tcp.corp.example";
    allow-update { domain-controllers; };
};

zone "_udp.corp.example" {
    type master;
    file "db._udp.corp.example";
    allow-update { domain-controllers; };
};
```

Discussion

The reason we can't allow dynamic updates to our main forward-mapping zone from our Domain Controllers is that it gives them too much control over the contents of the zone: someone could easily send—or spoof—dynamic updates from a Domain Controller and modify the zone. Instead, we create special subzones for the Domain Controllers to update. Since the domain names of the records they add usually end in _msdcs.corp.example, _sites.corp.example, _tcp.corp.example, or _udp.corp.example, the updates will modify the subzones, not their parent zone.

Domain Controllers do try to register two records that can cause problems, though: an A record attached to the domain name that matches the name of the Windows domain, and an A record in the _msdcs subdomain that has an underscore in the domain name. (All of the SRV records that Domain Controllers add have underscores in their domain names, but nearly all name servers allow that. BIND 8 name servers, by default, will complain about underscores in the owner of an A record, however.) To prevent the Domain Controller from trying to add these two records, change the value of the following Registry key to zero on the Domain Controllers:

HKEY_LOCAL_MACHINE\SYSTEM\CurrentControlSet\Services\Netlogon\Parameters
RegisterDNSARecords

See Also

"DNS and Windows 2000" in Chapter 16 of *DNS and BIND*; and "The Ties That BIND" in the March 2001 issue of Linux Magazine, at *http://www.linux-mag.com/2001-03/bind_01.html*.

8.9   Configuring a DHCP Server to Update a BIND Name Server

Problem

You want to configure the ISC DHCP server to update a BIND name server.

Solution

Within the *dhcpd.conf* file, add a *ddns-domainname* statement and a *ddns-rev-domainname* statement, if necessary. These define the name of the forward-mapping zone to add A records to and the suffix to append to inverted addresses to form the owner names of PTR records to add, respectively. The default *ddns-rev-domainname* is, naturally, *in-addr.arpa*. Here's an example:

```
ddns-domainname "foo.example";
ddns-rev-domainname "in-addr.arpa";
```

Next, add statements to specify the update style and whether the DHCP server should allow clients to update their own A records, if they wish. The recommended update style is "interim", which is described in this recipe. If you also want the DHCP server to handle all dynamic updates, add these statements:

```
ddns-update-style interim;
ignore client-updates;
```

Then define a TSIG key to use to sign updates. The syntax of the *key* statement is nearly identical to that used in the like-named statement in *named.conf*. Here's an example *key* statement:

```
key dhcp-server.foo.example. {
        algorithm hmac-md5;
        secret "R2xOu1NWXSPkvNqfP8Rm6Q==";
}
```

Note that there's no semicolon at the end of the statement (after "}").

Finally, add *zone* statements telling the DHCP server the domain names of the zones it will update, and for each of these, the address of the name server to send updates to and the TSIG key to sign those updates with. For example:

```
zone foo.example. {
        primary 127.0.0.1;
        key dhcp-server.foo.example.;
}

zone 0.168.192.in-addr.arpa. {
        primary 127.0.0.1;
        key dhcp-server.foo.example.;
}
```

Again, there's no semicolon at the end of the statement.

In this case, the DHCP server and the primary master name server for *foo.example* and *0.168.192.in-addr.arpa*—the zones the DHCP server needs to update—are running on the same host, so I specified the loopback address.

On the name server's side, use the newfangled *update-policy zone* substatement to limit which records the DHCP server's TSIG key can update. All the DHCP server should update in *foo.example* are A and TXT records, and never for the domain name of the zone. In the *0.168.192.in-addr.arpa* zone, the DHCP server should only update PTR records. These *zone* statements enforce those restrictions:

```
zone "foo.example" {
    type master;
    file "db.foo.example";
    update-policy {
        grant dhcp-server.foo.example. wildcard *.nxdomain.com. A TXT;
    };
};

zone "0.168.192.in-addr.arpa" {
    type master;
    file "db.192.168.0";
    update-policy {
        grant dhcp-server.foo.example. wildcard *.0.168.192.in-addr.arpa. PTR;
    };
};
```

For more information on *update-policy*, see Recipe 3.10.

Discussion

The 3.0 version of the ISC DHCP server supports sending dynamic updates. You can get a copy from *http://www.isc.org/products/DHCP/*.

When ignoring client updates, the DHCP server determines the domain name of the DHCP client by concatenating the first label of the domain name the client specifies in the FQDN option with the setting for the *ddns-domainname*.

The DHCP server needs to add TXT RRs to the forward-mapping zone because they're part of a clever mechanism it uses to avoid name collisions. When the DHCP initially adds an A record for a DHCP client, it computes a unique hash value for that client, based on the client's MAC address and other parameters. Then, it adds not just the A record to the client's domain name, but also a TXT record that contains the hash value.

Whenever the DHCP server needs to update a domain name's A record, it sets as a prerequisite that the domain name own a TXT record that matches the client's calculated hash value. If a TXT records exists with a different hash value, then another DHCP client is already using the same domain name.

See Also

dhcpd.conf(5), for more information on the syntax of *dhcpd.conf* and of the DHCP server's support for dynamic update; Recipe 3.10, for an explanation of *update-policy*.

CHAPTER 9

Resolvers and Programming

9.0   Introduction

Resolvers are considerably easier to configure than name servers. A BIND resolver supports just a few configuration directives:

domain
> Sets the resolver's local domain name

search
> Sets the resolver's search list and, implicitly, the local domain name

nameserver
> Configures the resolver to query a remote name server

sortlist
> Configures the resolver to sort certain A records to the beginning of responses

options
> Controls miscellaneous aspects of the resolver's configuration, such as timeouts

Windows resolvers support configuration of a similar set of parameters: at least the local domain name, search list, and remote name servers to query. This chapter includes recipes for configuring each of these aspects of a resolver's behavior, for both BIND and Windows resolvers. It also includes several sample programs that demonstrate how to use the invaluable Net::DNS module to send queries, request zone transfers, and send dynamic updates from a Perl program.

9.1   Configuring a Resolver to Query a Remote Name Server

Problem

You want to configure a resolver to query a name server running on a particular remote host.

Solution

On a host running a BIND resolver, add a *nameserver* directive to the *resolv.conf* file. The *resolv.conf* file (note that there's no "e" on the end of "resolv") usually lives in the */etc* directory; if it doesn't exist, create one with your favorite editor. Specify the address of the remote name server as the single argument to the *nameserver* directive. For example:

```
nameserver 192.168.0.1
```

You may also want to designate one or more name servers for the resolver to query if the first one doesn't respond, or if there's some error in sending the query to the first name server. To specify a backup name server, just add another *nameserver* directive with the backup name server's address as its argument:

```
nameserver 192.168.0.1
nameserver 192.168.0.2
```

The resolver queries the name servers in the order you list them in *resolv.conf*.

For a Windows resolver, find the resolver configuration window. On Windows 2000, for example, you can bring up the resolver configuration window by choosing *Start → Settings → Control Panel → Network and Dial-up Connections*. Right-click on the name of your network connection, select *Properties*, then double-click on *Internet Protocol (TCP/IP) Properties*. Check the box labeled *Use the following DNS server addresses* and fill in the address of the remote name server in the field labeled *Preferred DNS server*. Specify a backup name server, if you like, in the *Alternate DNS server* field.

Discussion

Configuring a resolver to use a backup name server is a good idea, since without a backup, a single name server's failure will cripple the resolver.

Resolvers send recursive queries by default, so make sure that the name server you configure a resolver to query will accept recursive queries from it.

See Also

"The nameserver Directive" and "Windows 2000" in Chapter 6 of *DNS and BIND*; "Name Servers to Query" in Chapter 6 of *DNS on Windows 2000.*.

9.2 Configuring a Resolver to Resolve Single-Label Domain Names

Problem

You want to configure a resolver so that it can resolve single-label domain names.

Solution

For a BIND resolver, configure the resolver's local domain name by adding a *domain* directive to *resolv.conf*. Specify the local domain name as the single argument to *domain*. For example:

```
domain foo.example
```

Now, when you use single-label domain names as arguments, the resolver will append the local domain name before looking them up.

With a Windows resolver, find the resolver configuration window and set the *Domain* (in Windows 95 or 98) or the *Primary DNS Suffix* (in Windows 2000 and Windows XP). To get to the right window in Windows 2000, right-click on *My Computer* and choose *Properties → Network Identification → Properties*.

Discussion

On most Unixish operating systems, setting the local domain name also determines how the OS interprets names that appear in system files, such as *.rhosts* and *hosts.equiv*. Single-label names in those files are assumed to end in the local domain name.

If you want to specify more than one domain name to append to domain name arguments, configure the resolver's search list, as shown in Recipe 9.3.

See Also

"The Local Domain Name" and "Windows 2000" in Chapter 6 of *DNS and BIND*; "DNS Suffix" in Chapter 6 of *DNS on Windows 2000*.

9.3   Configuring a Resolver to Append Multiple Domain Names to Arguments

Problem

You want to configure a resolver to append more than one domain name to incomplete domain name arguments.

Solution

On a BIND resolver, configure a search list by adding a *search* directive to the *resolv.conf* file. You can specify up to six domain names as arguments to the *search* directive, in the order in which you want the resolver to append them. For example, specifying:

```
search foo.example bar.example
```

tells your resolver to try appending *foo.example* to domain name arguments, and if that doesn't produce a real domain name, to try *bar.example*.

For a Windows resolver, find the resolver configuration window and set the *Domain Suffix Search Order*, Microsoft's term for the search list. In Windows 2000, for example, you can bring up the resolver configuration window by choosing *Start → Settings → Control Panel → Network and Dial-up Connections*. Right-click on the name of your network connection, select *Properties*, then double-click on *Internet Protocol (TCP/IP) Properties*. Finally, choose *Advanced → DNS....* Check the box labeled *Append these DNS suffixes (in order)*, and set the search list in the list box below.

Discussion

The *search* directive also sets the local domain name to its first argument, so be sure to delete any *domain* directive in *resolv.conf* when you add *search*.

See Also

"The Search List" and "Windows 2000" in Chapter 6 of *DNS and BIND*; "Search List" in Chapter 6 of *DNS on Windows 2000*.

9.4   Sorting Multiple Addresses in a Response

Problem

You want to configure a resolver to sort addresses on certain networks to the front of responses that include multiple A records.

Solution

For a BIND 4.9 or later resolver, add a *sortlist* directive to *resolv.conf*, telling the resolver which networks to prefer. The arguments to the *sortlist* directive are either network numbers or network and netmask pairs, separated by a slash ("/"). If you specify just a network number, the resolver assumes you mean the whole class A, B, or C network, as determined by the first two bits of the network. For example, given this *sortlist* directive, the resolver will sort addresses on the network 128.32/16 to the beginning of the list of addresses that it passes back to applications:

```
sortlist 128.32.0.0
```

If you specify a network and a netmask, use dotted-octet quantities for both. For example:

```
sortlist 10.1.0.0/255.255.0.0
```

Some Windows operating systems, including Windows NT 4.0 after Service Pack 4 and Windows 2000, also include resolvers that sort addresses, though the function isn't particularly configurable. When these resolvers share a subnet with the name server they query, they sort addresses on that subnet to the front of responses they return to applications.

You can turn address sorting off with these resolvers by setting the value of the following Registry key to zero:

```
HKEY_LOCAL_MACHINE\SYSTEM\CurrentControlSet\Services\Tcpip\Parameters \
PrioritizeRecordData
```

Discussion

Since most applications simple-mindedly use the first address returned before the rest, this configuration induces many applications to prefer addresses in the sortlist. Note, however, that in some cases the sortlist can also prevent round robin from working, since the resolver may sort responses that include matching addresses.

See Also

"The sortlist directive" in Chapter 6 of *DNS and BIND*; "Subnet Prioritization" in Chapter 6 of *DNS on Windows 2000*.

9.5   Changing the Resolver's Timeout

Problem

You want to change a resolver's timeout.

Solution

With a resolver based on BIND 8.2 or later code, use the *options timeout* directive in *resolv.conf*. The directive's argument is a timeout in seconds, separated from the keyword *timeout* with a colon. For example, to set the initial timeout to two seconds, you could add this directive to *resolv.conf*:

```
options timeout:2
```

The maximum value is 30 seconds; the minimum is 1 second.

The default timeout for the first round of queries is five seconds per name server. After each round of queries to the name servers listed in *resolv.conf*, the resolver doubles the initial timeout. BIND 8.2 and previous resolvers send a total of four rounds of queries; BIND 8.2.1 and later resolvers send two.

There is no way to modify the timeouts in a Windows resolver. However, the default timeouts are fairly short in newer Windows resolvers (one second for the first query in Windows 2000, for example), so adjusting them may not be necessary.

Discussion

If you're using a BIND 8.2 or later resolver, you may also find it useful to change the number of rounds of queries the resolver sends with *options attempts*. *options attempts* takes an integer number of attempts as an argument, after a colon. For example:

```
options attempts:1
```

Again, the default value is four up to BIND 8.2, and two thereafter. The maximum value for the option is five.

To specify multiple options, use a single *options* directive, like so:

```
options timeout:2 attempts:4
```

If you or your users are experiencing lots of timeouts, however, consider taking a close look at your name servers before monkeying with the resolver timeout. A correctly configured, reasonably loaded name server should be able to respond to nearly any query in less five seconds, assuming that the name servers authoritative for the zone that contains the answer are reachable and themselves correctly configured.

See Also

"The options Directive" in Chapter 6 of *DNS and BIND*; "Name Servers to Query" in Chapter 6 of *DNS on Windows 2000*.

9.6 Configuring the Order in Which a Resolver Uses DNS, /etc/hosts, and NIS

Problem

You want to configure the order in which a system's resolver consults various naming services.

Solution

Some vendor's BIND resolvers support configuration of the order in which the resolvers look up names using the various naming services they support. These naming services may include DNS, NIS, NIS+ and */etc/hosts*. On the Solaris and HP-UX operating systems, as well as recent versions of Linux and Irix, resolver service order is configured using the *nsswitch.conf* file, which usually resides in the */etc* directory. Lines in *nsswitch.conf* begin with the name of a *database*, followed by a colon and a list of one or more *sources*. For the resolver, the database name is *hosts*, and the possible sources are:

dns
> The name servers listed in *resolv.conf*

files
> */etc/hosts*

nis
> Sun's Network Information Service

nisplus
> Sun's NIS+

The resolver tries the sources in the order listed, so to tell the resolver to check */etc/hosts* before querying a name server, you could add this line to *nsswitch.conf*:

```
hosts: files dns
```

By default, the resolver continues to the next source if the previous isn't available or can't find a name. You can modify this behavior by adding *condition=action* clauses between source names. The possible conditions are:

unavail
> True if the previous source hasn't been configured (for example, for DNS, there's no local name server running and no *resolv.conf* file).

notfound
> True if a lookup using the previous source returns an answer that indicates that the name doesn't exist.

tryagain
> True if a lookup using the previous source indicates a temporary failure (for example, a DNS query timeout).

success
> True if a lookup using the previous source succeeds.

The supported actions are either *return* (return the result from the previous source) or *continue* (go on to the next source). The clause is written in square brackets:

```
hosts: files [notfound=continue] dns
```

On Windows 95, 98, and ME, you can configure resolver service order by adding subkeys to the following Registry key:

```
HKEY_LOCAL_MACHINE\System\CurrentControlSet\Services\VxD\MSTCP\ServiceProvider
```

The four Registry subkeys, each a signed, 16-bit number in hexadecimal format, control the order in which the Windows resolver uses the *HOSTS* and *LMHOSTS* files, name servers, and NBT queries to resolve names:

LocalPriority
> The LMHOSTS file, default priority 499

HostsPriority
> The HOSTS file, default priority 500

DNSPriority
> The configured name servers, default priority 2000

NetbtPriority
> NBT queries, default priority 2001

The lower the value of the key, the earlier the resolver uses that naming service. Deleting a subkey prevents the resolver from using the corresponding service.

Discussion

Some older versions of Linux support configuration of the service order using a file called *host.conf*; try *man host.conf* to see if your version does.

The only support in Windows NT 4.0 and Windows 2000 for configuring the service order is a single Registry key:

```
HKEY_LOCAL_MACHINE\SYSTEM\CurrentControlSet\Services\Tcpip\Parameters\
DnsNbtLookupOrder
```

The default value, 0, tells the resolver to query name servers before using NBT queries. Set the value to 1 to instruct the resolver to use NBT queries first.

See Also

"Vendor-Specific Options" in Chapter 6 of *DNS and BIND*.

9.7   Looking Up Records Programmatically

Problem

You want to look up resource records within a computer program.

Solution

One of the easiest ways to look up records programmatically is to use the Net::DNS Perl module, originally developed by Michael Fuhr and now maintained by Chris Reinhardt. You can get a copy of Net::DNS from *http://www.net-dns.org/*, or from CPAN.

Once you've installed Net::DNS, using it is easy. A program to look up a domain name's addresses could be as simple as this:

```perl
#!/usr/bin/perl -w

use Net::DNS;

# If the user didn't specify a domain name to look up, exit
die "Usage:  $0 <domain name>" unless (@ARGV == 1);

# Create a resolver object
my $res    = Net::DNS::Resolver->new;

# Look up A records (the default) for the domain name argument
my $query = $res->search($ARGV[0]);

# If this returned an answer...
if ($query) {

    # Print every A record in the answer message
    foreach my $rr ($query->answer) {
        next unless $rr->type eq "A";
        print $rr->address, "\n";
    }

# Otherwise print an error
} else {
    print "query failed: ", $res->errorstring, "\n";
}
```

Looking up other types of records only requires adding the type after the domain name argument; for example, changing the line of the script that calls *$res->search* to:

```perl
my $query = $res->search($ARGV[0], "MX");
```

And, naturally, you'd need to change the type of record you looked for in the *foreach* loop and what you printed when you found a record of the right type:

```perl
# Print every MX record in the answer message
foreach my $rr ($query->answer) {
    next unless $rr->type eq "MX";
    print $rr->string, "\n";
```

Discussion

There are lots of ways to look up records—both in Perl and in other programming languages. Choose whichever language you're most comfortable with: It's a good bet that it supports some method of querying name servers. For the fastest performance possible, you should probably use C. Chapter 15 of *DNS and BIND* describes how to use C's resolver routines to do simple DNS lookups.

See Also

The Net::DNS web site at *http://www.net-dns.org/*, and Chapter 15 of *DNS and BIND*.

9.8   Transferring a Zone Programmatically

Problem

You want to transfer a zone within a computer program.

Solution

One of the easiest ways to work with DNS programmatically is to use Perl's Net::DNS module, whether you're looking up discrete records or transferring an entire zone. Here's a short Perl script to transfer a zone specified on the command line and print the results:

```
#!/usr/bin/perl -w

use Net::DNS;

# If the user didn't specify the domain name of a zone and the domain name
# or address of a name server to transfer from, exit
die "Usage:  $0 <zone> <name server>" unless (@ARGV == 2);

# Create a resolver object
my $res  = Net::DNS::Resolver->new;

# Use the specified name server
$res->nameservers($ARGV[1]);

# Transfer the zone
my @zone = $res->axfr($ARGV[0]);

# Print each record in the zone
foreach $rr (@zone) {
        $rr->print;
}
```

Discussion

A more sophisticated script might require only the domain name of the zone, and would then look up the zone's NS records to find its authoritative name servers. And a more bulletproof script would do a whole lot more error checking.

Remember that you can only transfer a zone from a name server authoritative for that zone, and only if said name server allows you to. If you restrict zone transfers using TSIG, you can still use newer versions of Net::DNS to sign zone transfer requests. See Recipe 9.10 for details.

See Also

Recipe 9.10 for sending TSIG-signed requests.

9.9 Updating a Zone Programmatically

Problem

You want to dynamically update a zone programmatically.

Solution

I don't want to sound like a broken record, but here's another place where Net::DNS shines. Sending dynamic updates with the C resolver routines is fairly unpleasant. With Net::DNS, it's a breeze. Here's a script that uses dynamic update to add an A record for a host:

```perl
#!/usr/bin/perl -w

use Net::DNS;

# If the user didn't specify the domain name and address of a host to add, exit
die "Usage:  $0 <host> <address>" unless (@ARGV == 2);

my $host = $ARGV[0];
my $zone = $host;
my $addr = $ARGV[1];
my $primary;

# (Simplemindedly) Derive the domain name of the zone from the domain
# name of the host
$zone =~ s/^[\w-]+\.//;

# Create the update message
my $update = Net::DNS::Update->new($zone);

# Add an A records for the host
$update->push("update", rr_add("$host. 86400 A $addr"));
# Find the zone's primary master name server
my $res = Net::DNS::Resolver->new;
my $query = $res->query($zone, "SOA");

if ($query) {
        $primary = ($query->answer)[0]->mname;
```

```
        } else {
                die "Couldn't find primary master name server: ", $res->errorstring, "\n
";
        }

        $res->nameservers($primary);

        my $reply = $res->send($update);

        # Did it work?
        if (defined $reply) {
                if ($reply->header->rcode eq "NOERROR") {
                        print "Update succeeded\n";
                } else {
                        print "Update failed: ", $reply->header->rcode, "\n";
                }
        }
}
```

Discussion

As with the scripts in Recipes 9.7 and 9.8, this script doesn't do much input or error checking. Also, it could be more flexible: it could allow you to specify the TTL for the A record, and it could find the domain name of the zone to update by stripping off the labels of the domain name until it finds an SOA record, instead of just removing the first label and calling it a day.

Authorizing dynamic updates is a particularly apt use of TSIG. For help with signing dynamic updates with TSIG, see Recipe 9.10.

See Also

Recipe 5.19 for instructions on using *nsupdate* to send dynamic updates; Recipe 9.10 for sending TSIG-signed dynamic updates programmatically.

9.10 Signing Queries and Dynamic Updates with TSIG Programmatically

Problem

You want to use TSIG to sign a query or a dynamic update in Perl.

Solution

After you've used Net::DNS to create a query or an update to send, use the *sign_tsig* method to sign the query or update using that key. *sign_tsig* takes a key name and the base 64 encoding of the key's data as arguments. For example, to sign the update in the script in Recipe 9.9, you could replace this line of the script:

```
my $reply = $res->send($update);
```

With these lines:

```
$update->sign_tsig("update.key", "oyyvQvTOBTIcw7vvqvIJaQ==");

my $reply = $res->send($update);
```

You can also use TSIG to sign queries. Since the Net::DNS resolver's *axfr* method doesn't give you access to the query message, you must configure the resolver to sign all queries using the key before sending the AXFR query, rather than signing just the query. Here's a modified snippet of the script in Recipe 9.8 that shows one way to do that:

```
$tsig = Net::DNS::RR->new("tsig.key TSIG oyyvQvTOBTIcw7vvqvIJaQ==");
$res->tsig($tsig);

# Transfer the zone
my @zone = $res->axfr($ARGV[0]);
```

Discussion

Remember that the key's name and data must match in the script and on the name server that receives the query or update, and that the clocks on the sender of the message and on the name server that receives it must be synchronized within a few minutes of each other.

See Also

Recipe 7.9 for instructions on configuring a TSIG key, Recipe 7.10 for instructions on securing zone transfers with TSIG, and Recipe 3.10 for securing dynamic updates with *update-policy*.

## CHAPTER 10

Logging and Troubleshooting

10.0 Introduction

BIND name servers, particularly busy ones, can log a tremendous volume of messages. Many administrators are so cowed by the quantity of messages that they simply abandon trying to track them. Knowing how to sift and sort the messages, as described in Recipes 10.3 to 10.8, can help you keep up.

The recipes later in the chapter describe how to use *dig*, the Swiss Army Knife of DNS query tools. The latest versions of *dig* will trace name resolution, send TSIG-signed queries and more, all with a few command-line options.

10.1 Finding a Syntax Error in a named.conf File

Problem

You need to find a syntax error in a name server's *named.conf* file.

Solution

If you suspect you have a syntax error in *named.conf*, check the name server's *syslog* output to see if *named* logged any error messages the last time you started or reloaded it. Look for a message like this, indicating the last time you started the name server:

```
Jun 25 15:42:43 ns1 named[53702]: starting BIND 9.2.1
Jun 25 15:42:43 ns1 named[53702]: using 1 CPU
Jun 25 15:42:43 ns1 named[53702]: loading configuration from '/etc/named.conf'
```

If you reloaded the name server, the message will look like this:

```
Jun 25 15:44:25 ns1 named[53702]: loading configuration from '/etc/named.conf'
```

If you can't find the last time the name server was started or reloaded, you can always reload it again with *rndc reload* (BIND 9) or *ndc reload* (BIND 8), then check *named*'s *syslog* output immediately. Or you can start a BIND 9 name server with the *–g* option, which tells *named* to run in the foreground and send all error messages to standard error. For example:

```
$ named -g
Jun 25 15:53:37.745 starting BIND 9.2.1 -g
Jun 25 15:53:37.745 using 1 CPU
Jun 25 15:53:37.750 loading configuration from '/etc/named.conf'
Jun 25 15:53:37.750 /etc/named.conf:7: missing ';' before 'acl'
Jun 25 15:53:37.754 loading configuration: failure
Jun 25 15:53:37.754 exiting (due to fatal error)
```

This makes the error fairly obvious: there's a missing semicolon on line 7 of *named.conf*, before the keyword *acl*.

You can also check a *named.conf* file without running *named*, by using the BIND 9 *named-checkconf* program, as described in Recipe 5.2. *named-checkconf* uses the same routines that *named* would to check the *named.conf* file. For example, running *named-checkconf* on the *named.conf* file that produced the output above produces very similar output:

```
$ named-checkconf
/etc/named.conf:7: missing ';' before 'acl'
```

Discussion

While *named-checkconf* is not included in BIND 8 distributions—it was introduced in BIND 9.1.0—you can still build a BIND 9 *named-checkconf* and use it with a *named.conf* file meant for a BIND 8 name server. Just ignore any errors that tell you that the BIND 8-only configuration substatements you're using are obsolete:

```
$ named-checkconf
/etc/named.conf:29: option 'multiple-cnames' is obsolete
```

See Also

Recipe 5.2, for using *named-checkconf* to check a *named.conf* file.

10.2   Finding a Syntax Error in a Zone Data File

Problem

You need to find a syntax error in a zone data file.

Solution

Find the log messages from the most recent restart or reload of the name server, reloading again if necessary, as described in Recipe 10.1. Then look for a message indicating the line of the zone data file that contains the error. For example:

```
Jun 25 16:15:13 ns1 named[53941]: starting BIND 9.2.1
Jun 25 16:15:13 ns1 named[53941]: using 1 CPU
Jun 25 16:15:13 ns1 named[53941]: loading configuration from '/etc/named.conf'
Jun 25 16:15:13 ns1 named[53941]: listening on IPv4 interface fxp0, 192.168.0.1#53
Jun 25 16:15:13 ns1 named[53941]: listening on IPv4 interface lo0, 127.0.0.1#53
Jun 25 16:15:13 ns1 named[53941]: command channel listening on 0.0.0.0#953
Jun 25 16:15:13 ns1 named[53941]: dns_rdata_fromtext: db.foo.example:7: near eol:
unexpected end of input
Jun 25 16:15:13 ns1 named[53941]: zone foo.example/IN: loading master file db.foo.
example: unexpected end of input
Jun 25 16:15:13 ns1 named[53941]: running
```

And, of course, you can start your BIND 9 name server with –g to force it to run in the foreground and print errors to *stderr*.

If you'd rather not start a new *named* process, you can use the BIND 9 *named-checkzone* program, as described in Recipe 5.2. Like *named-checkconf*, *named-checkzone* is built with the same routines that *named* uses. To run it, specify the domain name of the zone and the name of the zone data file as arguments:

```
# named-checkzone foo.example db.foo.example
dns_rdata_fromtext: db.foo.example:7: near eol: unexpected end of input
zone foo.example/IN: loading master file db.foo.example: unexpected end of input
```

Discussion

Since the master file format didn't change between BIND 8 and BIND 9, you can also use *named-checkzone* on zone data files you load on your BIND 8 name server. The only difference you might encounter is that BIND 8 name servers can be configured to allow multiple CNAME records attached to the same domain name, while BIND 9 name servers can't.

See Also

Recipe 5.2, for using *named-checkzone* to check a zone data file.

10.3 Sending Log Messages to a Particular File

Problem

You want to send some or all of a name server's log messages to a particular file.

Solution

Add a *logging* statement to the name server's *named.conf* file, creating a new file log channel and sending output in one or more categories to that channel.

For example, to create a channel called *security_log* that writes logged messages to the file *security.log* in the name server's working directory, you could use this *logging* statement:

```
logging {
    channel security_log {
        file "security.log";
    };
};
```

By default, the channel logs any messages at severity *info* or higher. You can adjust this using the *severity* substatement:

```
logging {
    channel security_log {
        file "security.log";
        severity error;    // Query logging is at severity info
    };
};
```

This *logging* statement doesn't do anything useful yet, because no categories of messages are actually assigned to the channel. To specify a channel to send output in a particular category to, add a *category* substatement to your *logging* statement. For example:

```
logging {
    channel security_log {
        file "security.log";
    };

    category security { "security_log"; };
};
```

Both BIND 8 and BIND 9 categorize most messages they log, but they use different category names. See "Category Details" in Chapter 7 of *DNS and BIND* for a list. One difference that merits special mention is BIND 8's *default* category; in BIND 8, *default* includes both categories of messages not explicitly assigned to a channel *and* messages that aren't categorized. BIND 9 name servers still use the *default* category for the former purpose, but the new *general* category for the latter.

Discussion

By default, the name server will only log the message itself to the log channel. The *print-time channel* substatement tells the name server to print a timestamp before the logged message, which produces output like this:

```
Jun 26 15:49:41.554 client 192.168.0.1#1889: update foo.example/IN' denied
```

Here's how to set *print-time* in the *security_log* channel:

```
logging {
    channel security_log {
        file "security.log";
        severity error;    // Query logging is at severity info
        print-time yes;    // Print a timestamp with each message
    };
};
```

It's not always obvious which category a given message is assigned to. If you need to figure out the category a particular message is in, see Recipe 10.5.

See Also

Recipe 10.5 for determining the category of a message, Recipe 10.8 for setting up log file rotation, and "The Logging Statement" in Chapter 7 of *DNS and BIND*.

10.4   Discarding a Category of Messages

Problem

You want to discard all messages logged in a particular category.

Solution

Add a *category* substatement to the *logging* statement in the name server's *named.conf* file (or add a *logging* statement, if *named.conf* doesn't contain one), assigning the category to the *null* channel. For example, you can discard all messages about lame name servers with this *logging* statement:

```
logging {
    category lame-servers { null; };
};
```

Discussion

The *update-security* category, introduced in BIND 9.3.0, was created just so administrators could dump "Update denied" messages into the *null* channel without missing more important security-related messages.

See Also

Recipe 8.6, to stop Windows computers from trying to dynamically update a zone, Recipe 10.5, if you're not sure which category a message is in, and "The Logging Statement" in Chapter 7 of *DNS and BIND*.

10.5 Determining Which Category a Message Is In

Problem

You need to determine which logging category a particular message is in.

Solution

With a BIND 9 name server, add a *channel* substatement to the *logging* statement in *named.conf*, redefining the *default_syslog* channel so that the name server prints the category of all messages. For example:

```
logging {
    channel default_syslog {
        syslog daemon;          // usually the default
        print-category yes;
    };
};
```

Then wait for the message in question to reappear, or induce the name server to log it again. The name server will print the category of the message just before the message itself. For example:

```
Jun 26 16:31:56 ns1 named[62314]: general: loading configuration from '/etc/named.
conf'
```

This shows that this message is in the *general* category.

BIND 8 name servers won't let you redefine the *default_syslog* channel, so define a new *syslog* channel and assign the *default* category of messages to it:

```
logging {

    channel new_syslog {
        syslog daemon;
        print-category yes;
    };

    category default { new_syslog; };

};
```

Discussion

You can use the same technique to find out the severity a given message is logged at; just use the *print-severity* substatement instead of *print-category*.

See Also

"The Logging Statement" in Chapter 7 of *DNS and BIND*.

10.6 Sending syslog Output to Another Host

Problem

You want to send a name server's *syslog* output to another host.

Solution

Add a line to your host's *syslog.conf* file, telling *syslogd* to send messages logged in the facility the name server uses—usually *daemon*—to a remote host. For example, to send facility *daemon* messages to a remote host called *loghost.foo.example*, you could add this entry to *syslog.conf*:

```
daemon.info    @loghost.foo.example
```

Discussion

On the remote host, you may need to change *syslogd*'s command-line options to accept messages logged from the host that runs the name server. On some operating systems, you specify the address of a remote host that's allowed to log messages via *syslog* using *syslogd*'s *−a* command-line option. For example, to allow messages logged from the host at 192.168.0.1, you could start *syslogd* as:

```
# syslogd -a 192.168.0.1/32
```

To allow messages logged from any host on the 192.168.0/24 network, you could use:

```
# syslogd -a 192.168.0/24
```

To specify multiple addresses or networks, use multiple *−a* options.

If you just want to send *named*'s logged output to the remote host—not everything logged to the *daemon* facility—redefine the *default_syslog* channel to use one of the local facilities, *local0* to *local7*. For example:

```
logging {
    channel default_syslog {
        syslog local0;
    };
};
```

For a BIND 8 name server, you'll need to create a new *syslog* channel, as described in Recipe 10.5, since you can't redefine *default_syslog*.

Then add an entry to *syslog.conf* to send all messages in the facility to the remote host:

```
local0.*        @loghost.foo.example
```

Aggregating the *syslog* output from all of your BIND name servers on a single host can make monitoring those name servers much easier: you only have one *syslog* file to watch.

See Also

syslogd(8), *syslog.conf(5)*, and Recipe 10.5, for defining a new channel for default *syslog* messages.

10.7   Logging Dynamic Updates

Problem

You want to log the dynamic updates received by a name server.

Solution

By default, a name server will log dynamic updates it receives, both successful and failed, at severity *info*. For each successful dynamic update, you'll see a message like this in the name server's *syslog* output:

```
Jun 25 19:55:38 ns1 named[54132]: client 192.168.0.1#2206: updating zone 'foo.
example/IN': deleting an rrset
```

For each failed dynamic update, you'll see a message like this:

```
Jun 25 19:57:39 ns1 named[54132]: client 192.168.0.1#2213: update 'foo.example/IN'
denied
```

Or, for an update that failed because a prerequisite wasn't met, you'll see a message like this one:

```
Jun 25 20:00:02 ns1 named[54132]: client 192.168.0.1#2220: updating zone 'foo.
example/IN': update failed: 'name in use' prerequisite not satisfied (NXDOMAIN)
```

The first and last types of dynamic update messages are logged in the *update* category; the middle variety is logged in the *security* category. You can separate these messages from others by adding a *logging* statement to the name server's *named.conf* file that sends messages in each of these categories to special files. For example:

```
logging {

    channel update_log {
        file "update.log";
        severity info;
        print-time yes;
    };
```

```
channel security_log {
    file "security.log";
    severity info;
    print-time yes;
};

category update { update_log; };
category security { security_log; };

};
```

Discussion

If you don't see any messages in the *syslog* output, check the host's *syslog.conf* file and make sure *syslogd* is logging all messages at severity *info* or higher. *named* usually logs to the facility *daemon*, so an entry to log all of those messages might look like this:

```
daemon.info    /var/log/messages
```

Note that there are *many* different security-related messages in the *security* category, most of them unrelated to dynamic updates. In BIND 9.3.0, the name server separates update- from other security-related messages by placing "update denied" messages into *update-security* category.

As you can see from the messages cited so far in this recipe, the standard *syslog* messages about dynamic updates say very little about the contents of an update (that is, the change that the update made or tried to make), except the zone that the update tried to modify. To see the changes that were made, you'd have to look at the dynamic update log file. In BIND 8, the dynamic update log file is named after the zone data file, with *.log* on the end. In BIND 9, the file ends in *.jnl*. The *.log* file is in ASCII format and contains human-readable entries like this:

```
;BIND LOG V8
[DYNAMIC_UPDATE] id 56537 from [192.168.0.1].4662 at 1019882646 (named pid 21378):
zone:   origin foo.example class IN serial 2002042600
update: {add} test.foo.example 3600 IN A 10.0.0.93
```

These entries, significantly, include a timestamp that indicates when the update was processed; for this update, the timestamp is 1019882646, the number of seconds since the Unix epoch. To convert that to a date and time, you can use the *date* command:

```
$ date -r 1019882646
Fri Apr 26 22:44:06 MDT 2002
```

The timestamp may help you correlate this change with a particular message from the name server's *syslog* output.

The *.jnl* file is in a binary format. To decipher it, build the *journalprint* program from the BIND distribution:

```
$ cd bin/tests
$ make journalprint
```

To run *journalprint*, just specify the journal file you want to decode as the argument:

```
$ journalprint db.foo.example.jnl
del foo.example.                86400   IN      SOA     ns1.foo.example. root.foo.
example. 2002062500 3600 900 2592000 3600
add foo.example.                86400   IN      SOA     ns1.foo.example. root.foo.
example. 2002062501 3600 900 2592000 3600
add mail.foo.example.   3600    IN      A       192.168.0.2
add foo.example.                3600    IN      MX      0 mail.foo.example.
add foo.example.                3600    IN      TXT     "Test update"
```

The lines that begin with *del* indicate records deleted, while lines that begin with *add*... well, you get the idea. You'll see the zone's SOA record being added and deleted with every update: that's actually just the serial number incrementing automatically.

Since there's no timestamp in the journal file, it's not generally possible to correlate individual changes with particular *syslog* messages.

See Also

Recipe 3.10, for allowing dynamic updates to a zone.

10.8   Rotating Log Files

Problem

You want to rotate a name server's log files.

Solution

BIND name servers support a limited form of log file rotation. When you define a file channel, you can specify that the name server keep some number of versions of the file with the *versions* argument to the *file* substatement. For example, this channel definition tells the name server to save seven versions of the *named.log* file:

```
logging {
    channel "named_log" {
        file "named.log" versions 7;
        print-time yes;
    };
};
```

The name server will only rotate the files when it's restarted or reloaded, so after seven restarts or reloads, you'll have a *named.log*, *named.log.1*, and so on.

You can combine the *versions* argument with the *size* argument to tell the name server to rotate the log file once it reaches a certain size. For example, to rotate the log file once it reaches a megabyte in size, you could use this *channel* substatement:

```
logging {
    channel "named_log" {
        file "named.log" versions 7 size 1m;
        print-time yes;
    };
};
```

Discussion

With a size specified, log files are only renamed when the current log file exceeds the size limit, not on restart or reload.

Use the keyword *unlimited* to keep an unlimited number of old versions of a log file:

```
logging {
    channel "named_log" {
        file "named.log" versions unlimited size 1m;
        print-time yes;
    };
};
```

On BIND 8, *unlimited* is actually synonymous with "99" for purposes of log file rotation.

See Also

"The Logging Statement" in Chapter 7 of *DNS and BIND*.

10.9 Looking Up Records with dig

Problem

You want to look up records using *dig*.

Solution

Specify the domain name you want to look up, the record type you're interested in (unless it's A, the default), and the domain name or IP address of the name server you want to query (unless it's the first one in your resolver's configuration, which is the default) as arguments to *dig*:

```
$ dig @a.gtld-servers.net a www.oreilly.com
```

The arguments may appear in any order: *dig* is smart enough to determine which is which (fairly easy, since the name server's domain name or address has an "@" in front of it, domain names usually have dots in them, and there are only so many record types).

Unlike *nslookup*, *dig* doesn't apply the search list by default, so use fully qualified domain names, both to specify the domain name you want to look up and any remote name server you want to query.

Discussion

dig prints the DNS response message it gets back in a very detailed format. For example, here's the output produced by the *dig* command above:

```
; <<>> DiG 9.2.1 <<>> @a.gtld-servers.net www.oreilly.com a
;; global options:  printcmd
;; Got answer:
;; ->>HEADER<<- opcode: QUERY, status: NOERROR, id: 17064
;; flags: qr rd; QUERY: 1, ANSWER: 0, AUTHORITY: 2, ADDITIONAL: 2

;; QUESTION SECTION:
;www.oreilly.com.               IN      A

;; AUTHORITY SECTION:
oreilly.com.            172800  IN      NS      NS.oreilly.com.
oreilly.com.            172800  IN      NS      NS1.SONIC.NET.

;; ADDITIONAL SECTION:
NS.oreilly.com.         172800  IN      A       209.204.146.21
NS1.SONIC.NET.          172800  IN      A       208.201.224.11

;; Query time: 80 msec
;; SERVER: 192.5.6.30#53(a.gtld-servers.net)
;; WHEN: Thu Jun 27 16:49:31 2002
;; MSG SIZE  rcvd: 109
```

In this case, the answer is a little hard to find. The banner, on the first line, echoes the query sent (for A records for *www.oreilly.com* on *a.gtld-servers.net*). *dig* also prints the header (after ->>*HEADER*<<-), which tells us that this was a standard *QUERY* response (not a NOTIFY message or dynamic update), and that the return code was *NOERROR*, indicating that the query was processed successfully.

The rest of the header shows us that this was a nonauthoritative (*aa* didn't appear as a flag) response (*qr* was set). The query was recursive (*rd* means "recursion desired") but recursion wasn't available (*ra* didn't appear as a flag). That's not surprising, since we sent the query to a gTLD name server.

The *QUESTION SECTION* parrots the question we asked (again), and the *AUTHORITY SECTION* shows the two NS records returned by the name server we queried, referring us to name servers closer to the answer. The *ADDITIONAL SECTION* gives us the addresses of those name servers.

At the end, we see that the response took 80 milliseconds, that the name server we queried was *a.gtld-servers.net* at 192.5.6.30, plus a date- and timestamp and the fact that the reply was 109 bytes long.

If the name server we queried had actually returned the records we asked for, those records would appear in the answer section, as shown here:

```
$ dig @ns.oreilly.com www.oreilly.com a

; <<>> DiG 9.2.1 <<>> @ns.oreilly.com www.oreilly.com a
;; global options:  printcmd
;; Got answer:
;; ->>HEADER<<- opcode: QUERY, status: NOERROR, id: 40642
;; flags: qr aa rd ra; QUERY: 1, ANSWER: 1, AUTHORITY: 3, ADDITIONAL: 3

;; QUESTION SECTION:
;www.oreilly.com.                IN      A

;; ANSWER SECTION:
www.oreilly.com.        7200    IN      A       209.204.146.22

;; AUTHORITY SECTION:
oreilly.com.            7200    IN      NS      ns.oreilly.com.
oreilly.com.            7200    IN      NS      ns1.sonic.net.
oreilly.com.            7200    IN      NS      ns2.sonic.net.

;; ADDITIONAL SECTION:
ns.oreilly.com.         7200    IN      A       209.204.146.21
ns1.sonic.net.          6237    IN      A       208.201.224.11
ns2.sonic.net.          62511   IN      A       208.201.224.33

;; Query time: 100 msec
;; SERVER: 209.204.146.21#53(ns.oreilly.com)
;; WHEN: Thu Jun 27 16:55:01 2002
;; MSG SIZE  rcvd: 159
```

This time, it's an authoritative answer (*aa* is in the flags field) and recursion was available (the *ra* flag—whoops) and the A record we asked for is in the *ANSWER SECTION*.

See Also

dig(1) and "Using dig" in Chapter 12 of *DNS and BIND*.

10.10 Reverse-Mapping an Address with dig

Problem

You want to reverse-map an address to a domain name using *dig*.

Solution

Use *dig*'s *-x* command-line option, which takes an IP address as an option argument. For example:

```
$ dig -x 209.204.146.22
```

dig prints the interpreted DNS response message, just as it did in Recipe 10.9:

```
; <<>> DiG 9.2.1 <<>> -x 209.204.146.22
;; global options:  printcmd
;; Got answer:
;; ->>HEADER<<- opcode: QUERY, status: NOERROR, id: 12896
;; flags: qr rd ra; QUERY: 1, ANSWER: 1, AUTHORITY: 2, ADDITIONAL: 0

;; QUESTION SECTION:
;22.146.204.209.in-addr.arpa.   IN      PTR

;; ANSWER SECTION:
22.146.204.209.in-addr.arpa. 21600 IN  PTR     www.oreilly.com.

;; AUTHORITY SECTION:
146.204.209.in-addr.arpa. 21600 IN     NS      ns.oreilly.com.
146.204.209.in-addr.arpa. 21600 IN     NS      ns1.sonic.net.

;; Query time: 62 msec
;; SERVER: 192.168.0.1#53(192.168.0.1)
;; WHEN: Thu Jun 27 20:28:41 2002
;; MSG SIZE  rcvd: 118
```

The domain name the address maps to is shown in the *ANSWER SECTION*, as the RDATA of the PTR record (*www.oreilly.com*, in this case).

Discussion

If the PTR record reverse-mapping the address is in a zone delegated using the scheme described in RFC 2317 (Recipe 6.4), you may need to specify the type PTR on the command line, too: older versions of *dig* send queries for records in any type when you use the *-x* option. You can tell which variety your *dig* is by looking at the type of the query in the *QUESTION SECTION*. The version of *dig* we used in this recipe was a newer one, which sends an explicit PTR query.

You can also use *dig*'s *-x* option just to build the domain name to look up from the octets of the IP address and specify a different record type on the command line. For example, to look up A records attached to *0.168.192.in-addr.arpa* (read RFC 1101 for why you'd ever want to do that), you could use:

```
$ dig -x 192.168.0 a
```

See Also

dig(1); Recipe 6.4; RFCs 1101 and 2317; "Using dig" in Chapter 12 of *DNS and BIND*.

10.11 Transferring a Zone Using dig

Problem

You want to transfer a zone using *dig*.

Solution

Run *dig* as described in Recipe 10.9, specifying the domain name of the zone you want to transfer, the domain name or IP address of a name server authoritative for that zone, and the type *axfr*. For example:

```
$ dig @ns1.foo.example axfr foo.example
```

dig will print the results of the zone transfer:

```
; <<>> DiG 9.2.1 <<>> @ns1.foo.example axfr foo.example
;; global options:  printcmd
foo.example.            86400   IN      SOA     ns1.foo.example. root.foo.example.
2002062502 3600 900 2592000 3600
foo.example.            86400   IN      NS      ns1.foo.example.
foo.example.            3600    IN      MX      0 mail.foo.example.
mail.foo.example.       3600    IN      A       192.168.0.2
ns1.foo.example.        86400   IN      A       192.168.0.1
foo.example.            86400   IN      SOA     ns1.foo.example. root.foo.example.
2002062502 3600 900 2592000 3600
;; Query time: 183 msec
;; SERVER: 192.168.0.1#53(ns1.foo.example)
;; WHEN: Fri Jun 28 11:05:20 2002
;; XFR size: 7 records
```

Discussion

The SOA record appears twice in the output because name servers use a zone's SOA record to delimit the beginning and the end of the transfer.

You'll only be able to transfer zones from name servers that are authoritative for those zones, of course, and that allow zone transfers from the address of the host you're running *dig* on. If you try to transfer a zone from a name server that won't allow zone transfers from your address, you'll see output like this:

```
$ dig @ns1.foo.example axfr bar.example

; <<>> DiG 9.2.1 <<>> @ns1.foo.example axfr bar.example
;; global options:  printcmd
; Transfer failed.
```

Finally, if the name server you're trying to transfer the zone from uses TSIG to secure transfers, you can use *dig*'s *–k* command-line option to sign the query. With a BIND 9 version of *dig*, you can use the *–k* or *–y* command-line options. See Recipe 5.22 for

---

how to use *–k* and *–y*; it's exactly the same for BIND 8 and 9 versions of *dig* as it is for the corresponding versions of *nsupdate*.

See Also

dig(1); Recipe 5.22, for specifying a TSIG key with *–k* or *–y*; Recipe 7.10, for securing zone transfers; and "Zone Transfers with dig" in Chapter 12 of *DNS and BIND*.

10.12 Tracing Name Resolution Using dig

Problem

You want to trace the process of name resolution using *dig*.

Solution

Starting with a root name server, send nonrecursive queries (with the *+norec* command-line option) for the records you're looking for. (The root name servers are named *[a-m].root-servers.net*.) For example:

```
$ dig @a.root-servers.net www.oreilly.com +norec

; <<>> DiG 9.2.1 <<>> @a.root-servers.net www.oreilly.com +norec
;; global options:  printcmd
;; Got answer:
;; ->>HEADER<<- opcode: QUERY, status: NOERROR, id: 44699
;; flags: qr; QUERY: 1, ANSWER: 0, AUTHORITY: 13, ADDITIONAL: 13

;; QUESTION SECTION:
;www.oreilly.com.               IN      A

;; AUTHORITY SECTION:
com.                    172800  IN      NS      A.GTLD-SERVERS.NET.
com.                    172800  IN      NS      G.GTLD-SERVERS.NET.
com.                    172800  IN      NS      H.GTLD-SERVERS.NET.
com.                    172800  IN      NS      C.GTLD-SERVERS.NET.
com.                    172800  IN      NS      I.GTLD-SERVERS.NET.
com.                    172800  IN      NS      B.GTLD-SERVERS.NET.
com.                    172800  IN      NS      D.GTLD-SERVERS.NET.
com.                    172800  IN      NS      L.GTLD-SERVERS.NET.
com.                    172800  IN      NS      F.GTLD-SERVERS.NET.
com.                    172800  IN      NS      J.GTLD-SERVERS.NET.
com.                    172800  IN      NS      K.GTLD-SERVERS.NET.
com.                    172800  IN      NS      E.GTLD-SERVERS.NET.
com.                    172800  IN      NS      M.GTLD-SERVERS.NET.

;; ADDITIONAL SECTION:
A.GTLD-SERVERS.NET.     172800  IN      A       192.5.6.30
G.GTLD-SERVERS.NET.     172800  IN      A       192.42.93.30
```

```
H.GTLD-SERVERS.NET.      172800  IN      A       192.54.112.30
C.GTLD-SERVERS.NET.      172800  IN      A       192.26.92.30
I.GTLD-SERVERS.NET.      172800  IN      A       192.43.172.30
B.GTLD-SERVERS.NET.      172800  IN      A       192.33.14.30
D.GTLD-SERVERS.NET.      172800  IN      A       192.31.80.30
L.GTLD-SERVERS.NET.      172800  IN      A       192.41.162.30
F.GTLD-SERVERS.NET.      172800  IN      A       192.35.51.30
J.GTLD-SERVERS.NET.      172800  IN      A       210.132.100.101
K.GTLD-SERVERS.NET.      172800  IN      A       192.52.178.30
E.GTLD-SERVERS.NET.      172800  IN      A       192.12.94.30
M.GTLD-SERVERS.NET.      172800  IN      A       192.55.83.30

;; Query time: 84 msec
;; SERVER: 198.41.0.4#53(a.root-servers.net)
;; WHEN: Fri Jun 28 11:53:41 2002
;; MSG SIZE  rcvd: 465
```

When you receive a referral (a response with a *NOERROR* status, no answer section, and NS records in the authority section), send your next query to one of the name servers in the authority section. We'll query *m.gtld-servers.net* next:

```
$ dig @m.gtld-servers.net www.oreilly.com +norec

; <<>> DiG 9.2.1 <<>> @m.gtld-servers.net www.oreilly.com +norec
;; global options:  printcmd
;; Got answer:
;; ->>HEADER<<- opcode: QUERY, status: NOERROR, id: 53652
;; flags: qr; QUERY: 1, ANSWER: 0, AUTHORITY: 2, ADDITIONAL: 2

;; QUESTION SECTION:
;www.oreilly.com.               IN      A

;; AUTHORITY SECTION:
oreilly.com.            172800  IN      NS      NS.oreilly.com.
oreilly.com.            172800  IN      NS      NS1.SONIC.NET.

;; ADDITIONAL SECTION:
NS.oreilly.com.         172800  IN      A       209.204.146.21
NS1.SONIC.NET.          172800  IN      A       208.201.224.11

;; Query time: 251 msec
;; SERVER: 192.55.83.30#53(m.gtld-servers.net)
;; WHEN: Fri Jun 28 12:06:26 2002
;; MSG SIZE  rcvd: 109
```

Now we'll query *ns.oreilly.com*:

```
$ dig @ns.oreilly.com www.oreilly.com +norec

; <<>> DiG 9.2.1 <<>> @ns.oreilly.com www.oreilly.com +norec
;; global options:  printcmd
;; Got answer:
;; ->>HEADER<<- opcode: QUERY, status: NOERROR, id: 36079
;; flags: qr aa ra; QUERY: 1, ANSWER: 1, AUTHORITY: 3, ADDITIONAL: 2
```

```
;; QUESTION SECTION:
;www.oreilly.com.              IN      A

;; ANSWER SECTION:
www.oreilly.com.      7200    IN      A       209.204.146.22

;; AUTHORITY SECTION:
oreilly.com.          7200    IN      NS      ns2.sonic.net.
oreilly.com.          7200    IN      NS      ns.oreilly.com.
oreilly.com.          7200    IN      NS      ns1.sonic.net.

;; ADDITIONAL SECTION:
ns.oreilly.com.       7200    IN      A       209.204.146.21
ns2.sonic.net.        80335   IN      A       208.201.224.33

;; Query time: 254 msec
;; SERVER: 209.204.146.21#53(ns.oreilly.com)
;; WHEN: Fri Jun 28 12:07:01 2002
;; MSG SIZE  rcvd: 143
```

This response has the record we were after in the answer section, so we're done.

Discussion

Notice that the query doesn't change: in this example, we look up A records for *www.oreilly.com* each time. By following the referrals, we get closer and closer to the name servers authoritative for the zone that contains the answer.

BIND 9's version of *dig* has a command-line option to trace name resolution automatically—very slick! To reproduce the output above, you only need to run:

```
$ dig +trace www.oreilly.com
```

dig starts by looking up the list of root name servers on your default name server, then sends a nonrecursive query to one of them for the records you specified on the command line. Then it follows referrals, as we did, until it finds an answer.

If you're trying to track down a problem, not just reenacting name resolution for personal or pedagogical reasons, pay careful attention to *dig*'s output. Look for responses that indicate that the domain name doesn't exist (NXDOMAIN in the *status* field of the header) or that refer you to name servers authoritative for a zone higher up in the namespace (for example, an *oreilly.com* name server referring you to a *com* name server), which is a symptom of a lame delegation.

See Also

dig(1); and Recipe 6.5, for using *dig*'s *+trace* option to check delegation.

## CHAPTER 11

IPv6

11.0 Introduction

IPv6 is tomorrow's internetwork protocol—perennially, it seems. BIND has supported IPv6 forward and reverse-mapping since Version 4.9.5, released way back in 1996. BIND 9, finally, added support for IPv6 as a transport, responding to queries received over IPv6.

The IETF—the body that develops extensions to DNS, among other things—briefly flirted with a very complex method of handling IPv6 forward and reverse-mapping, using A6 and DNAME records and "bitstring labels." (Unfortunately, I wrote the fourth edition of *DNS and BIND* at just the wrong time and documented A6 and the rest.) Eventually, however, they opted to standardize on a system that uses AAAA and PTR records in a straightforward way, similar to the way A and PTR records work with IPv4 addresses.

11.1 Configuring a Name Server to Listen for Queries on an IPv6 Interface

Problem

You want a BIND 9 name server to listen for queries on an IPv6 interface.

Solution

Use the *listen-on-v6 options* substatement to instruct the name server to listen on any of the host's IPv6 interfaces for queries. For example:

```
options {
    directory "/var/named";
    listen-on-v6 { any; };
};
```

Don't specify the particular IPv6 address of one of the host's interfaces: *listen-on-v6* only supports *any* or *none* as an argument. The default, as of BIND 9.1.0, is *none*; that is, don't listen for queries on any IPv6 interfaces.

Discussion

Before BIND 9.1.0, BIND 9 name servers listened on any of the host's IPv6 interfaces by default. BIND 8 name servers can't handle queries received via IPv6 at all.

As with its IPv4 counterpart, you can use *listen-on-v6* to tell a name server to listen on an alternate port, too. For example, you could configure the name server to listen on port 1053 for IPv6 queries with:

```
options {
    directory "/var/named";
    listen-on-v6 port 1053 { any; };
};
```

Note that none of the root name servers have IPv6 interfaces, which makes it difficult to run an IPv6-only name server on the Internet. Typically, name servers with IPv6 interfaces also have at least one IPv4 interface, or forward to a name server that has both kinds.

See Also

"Configuring the IPv6 Transport" in Chapter 10 of *DNS and BIND*.

11.2 Configuring a Name Server to Send Queries from a Particular IPv6 Address

Problem

You want a BIND 9 name server to send queries from a particular IPv6 address.

Solution

Use the *query-source-v6 options* substatement to tell the name server to use a particular IPv6 address as the source address for queries it sends (over IPv6). For example, to use the address 222:10:2521:1:210:4bff:fe10:d24 as the source address for IPv6 queries, you could use:

```
options {
    directory "/var/named";
    query-source-v6 address 222:10:2521:1:210:4bff:fe10:d24;
};
```

Discussion

Only BIND 9 name servers can handle an IPv6 transport, so don't try this with a BIND 8 name server.

You can specify a particular source port to use for IPv6 queries by using the *port* argument. For example:

```
options {
    directory "/var/named";
    query-source-v6 address 222:10:2521:1:210:4bff:fe10:d24 port 5353;
};
```

There are also IPv6 counterparts to the *transfer-source* and *notify-source* substatements called, predictably, *transfer-source-v6* and *notify-source-v6*, respectively. The syntax is the same as the syntax of *query-source-v6* substatement, minus the *address* keyword. For example:

```
zone "foo.example" {
    type slave;
    masters { 222:10:2521:1:210:4bff:fe10:d24; };
    file "bak.foo.example";
    transfer-source-v6 222:10:2521:1:210:4c00:fe11:d22;
};
```

See Also

"Configuring the IPv6 Transport" in Chapter 10 of *DNS and BIND*.

11.3 Adding a Host with an IPv6 Interface

Problem

You need to add forward- and reverse-mapping records for a host with an IPv6 interface.

Solution

Add a AAAA (pronounced "quad A") record to the host's domain name, mapping the name to the host's IPv6 address. The RDATA of the AAAA record is an IPv6 address represented as eight groups of as many as four hexidecimal digits, separated by colons. For example:

```
0123:4567:89ab:cdef:0123:4567:89ab:cdef
```

Groups of hex digits that begin with one or more zeroes can be written without the zeroes, so that address could also be written as 123:4567:89ab:cdef:123:4567:89ab:cdef.

So a complete AAAA record might look like this:

```
host-v6.foo.example.  IN  AAAA  123:4567:89ab:cdef:123:4567:89ab:cdef
```

To reverse map the address back to a domain name, create a reverse-mapping zone under *ip6.arpa* to correspond to the network the host is on. Each label to the left of *ip6.arpa* corresponds to a nibble (four bits) of the 128-bit IPv6 address, written (as it was in the AAAA record's RDATA) as a hex digit. As with reverse-mapping zones for IPv4, the labels are written in the domain name in the opposite order as the corresponding bits appear in the address. So if you run the network 123:4567:89ab:cdef/64, you'd create a zone called *f.e.d.c.b.a.9.8.7.6.5.4.3.2.1.0.ip6.arpa*. (When creating domain names from IPv6 addresses, you do need to include every nibble of the address; you can't omit any zeroes.)

Within this zone, add a PTR record to the domain name formed by all 32 (!) of the nibbles in the host's IPv6 address, in reverse order, with *ip6.arpa* appended. So the PTR record that corresponds to the AAAA record shown earlier in this recipe would be:

```
f.e.d.c.b.a.9.8.7.6.5.4.3.2.1.0.f.e.d.c.b.a.9.8.7.6.5.4.3.2.1.0.ip6.arpa.  IN  PTR
host-v6.foo.example.
```

This is clearly a good time to take advantage of the default origin in the zone data file (the domain name of the zone), and abbreviate that to:

```
f.e.d.c.b.a.9.8.7.6.5.4.3.2.1.0    IN    PTR    host-v6.foo.example.
```

Discussion

You'll need to have your IPv6 reverse-mapping zone delegated to you, just like you had a subdomain of *in-addr.arpa* delegated to you in Recipe 1.71.7. Unless you work for an ISP, the ISP that assigned your IPv6 address space to you will probably delegate your IPv6 reverse-mapping zone to you, too. If you do work for an ISP, you may need to contact one of the address registries listed in Recipe 1.71.7 and ask them to delegate your IPv6 reverse-mapping zone to you.

You can test IPv6 forward- and reverse-mappings with *dig*. To look up the AAAA record above, you could run:

```
$ dig host-v6.foo.example aaaa
```

To look up the PTR record with a BIND 8.3.2 or later version of *dig*, you could use:

```
$ dig -x 123:4567:89ab:cdef:123:4567:89ab:cdef
```

To look up the PTR record with an older BIND 8 or a BIND 9 version of *dig*, you'd have to use:

```
$ dig ptr f.e.d.c.b.a.9.8.7.6.5.4.3.2.1.0.f.e.d.c.b.a.9.8.7.6.5.4.3.2.1.0.ip6.arpa
```

See Also

Recipe 1.71.7 for delegation of a reverse-mapping zone, RFC 1886 for the specification of the AAAA record and *ip6.int* (which is now *ip6.arpa*), and "IPv6 Forward and Reverse Mapping" in Chapter 10 of *DNS and BIND*.

11.4 Configuring rndc to Work Over IPv6

Problem

You want to use *rndc* over IPv6.

Solution

On a BIND 9.2.0 or later name server, add an *inet controls* statement to *named.conf*, telling the name server to listen on the host's IPv6 interface for control messages. For example:

```
controls {
    inet 123:4567:89ab:cdef:123:4567:89ab:cdef allow { any; } keys { "rndc-key"; };
};
```

Then specify the host's IPv6 address as the argument to *rndc*'s *−s* option, as in:

```
# rndc -s 123:4567:89ab:cdef:123:4567:89ab:cdef status
```

If you would like to make that address the default for *rndc* to connect to, add a *default-server options* substatement to *rndc.conf*, like this:

```
options {
    default-server 123:4567:89ab:cdef:123:4567:89ab:cdef;
    default-key "rndc-key";
};
```

Discussion

If you don't want to rely entirely on IPv6 for the name server's control channel, you can use multiple *inet controls* substatements. For example:

```
controls {
    inet * allow { localhost; } keys { "rndc-key"; };
    inet 123:4567:89ab:cdef:123:4567:89ab:cdef allow { any; } keys { "rndc-key"; };
};
```

As with *listen-on-v6*, introduced in Recipe 11.1, you can't use the predefined *localhost* or *localnets* ACLs with an IPv6 interface in the *controls* statement.

See Also

Recipe 11.1.

Index

Symbols

<> (angle brackets), 23
* (asterisk), 50, 71
@ (at sign), 24, 26, 35
{} (curly braces), 16, 48, 87
$ (dollar sign), 43
. (dot), 24, 25, 35
" (double quotes), 16, 48
() parentheses, 25
; (semicolon), 48, 165
/ (slash), 50, 171
[] (square brackets), 23
_ (underscore), 54, 164

A

A records
    abbreviating, 27
    adding programmatically, 178
    adding with nsupdate command, 116
    anti-spam tests, 93
    delegating subdomains, 125
    DHCP servers, 167
    disabling glue fetching, 141
    Domain Controllers, 164
    domain names, 44, 45
    dynamic updates, 61
    filtering host tables, 47
    hosts, 26, 34, 42
    mail servers, 45
    moving name servers, 132
    name resolution, 198
    pointing to URLs, 30
    pointing to web servers, 29, 30
    RDATA subfields, 23

    returning answer example, 72
    reverse-mapping zones, 126
    root name servers, 83, 84
    round robins, 31
    sortlists, 85, 86
    stub zones, 67
    TTLs, 33, 40
    underscores, 164
    web browsers, 91
    wildcard domain names, 85
A6 records, 158, 199
AAAA records, 43, 199, 201, 202
ACLs (access control lists)
    allow substatement, 52
    BIND 9, 48
    localhost or localnets, 203
    naming considerations, 148
    options statement and, 15
    queries, 149
    responses dependent on addresses, 70
    slaves with multiple views, 76
    zone transfers, 148
Active Directory, 163–165
additional-from-auth substatement, 59, 60
address keyword, 201
addresses
    looking up, 176
    regional registries, 8
    sorting multiple, 171
    (see also email address; IP addresses)
AirNav (Airport Information), 46
Airport Information (AirNav), 46
aliases
    adding, 27, 28
    CNAME record dictum, 30

We'd like to hear your suggestions for improving our indexes. Send email to *index@oreilly.com*.

chroot( ) environment, 21, 143, 144
class field, 33, 43
classes, 71, 99, 101
clients, 112, 113, 114
CNAME records
    BIND 4, 155
    delegating reverse-mapping, 128, 129
    domain names, 45, 123
    functionality, 27, 28
    $GENERATE control statement, 43
    mail servers and, 45
    pointing to URLs, 31
    pointing to web servers, 30
    wildcard domain names and, 42
com domain, 6
compilation options, 14, 15
concatenation, 24, 166
condition=action clauses, 174
configuration files
    BIND 8/9 formats, 156
    checking, 96
    rndc-confgen program, 51
    starting named automatically, 21
configure program, 13
configuring
    anti-spam tests and, 93
    backup mail servers, 89, 90
    based on mail routing, 91, 92
    BIND 4 slave accommodation, 157, 158
    BIND name servers, 48
    BIND Users mailing list, 2
    caching-only name servers, 142, 143
    finding closest servers, 85–87
    IXFRs, 79
    mail servers, 29
    multiple mail servers, 90, 91
    name servers, 49–54
        with firewalls, 137–138
        for forwarding, 62, 63, 67, 68
        to forward queries, 66, 67
        to listen, 80
        for not forwarding, 68, 69
        for zones, 15
    naming services order, 173–175
    primary masters for zones, 16, 17
    resolvers, 168, 169, 170, 171
    slave name servers, 57, 58
    slaves for zones, 17, 18
    stealth slaves, 140
    testing and, 82, 95–96
    for virtual email addresses, 92
Conrad, Lee, 93

control channels, 49–54, 96, 203
    (see also inet control channel; unix
        control channel)
control messages
    default ports for, 50
    file descriptors and, 112
    key statement and, 53
    listening for, 52
    rndc and, 103
    rndc over IPv6, 203
controls statement
    adding, 53
    BIND versions, 156
    configuring name servers, 49, 51, 52
    controlling multiple processes, 104
    controlling named processes, 103
    inet substatement, 49, 203
    setting up rndc, 20
    testing configuration, 96
conversion, date/time, 189
country-code top-level domains (see ccTLDs)
Cricket's Corner, 2
cryptography, 146
curly braces ({}), 16, 48, 87
cyclic order, 71, 72

D

daemon facility, 11, 187, 189
data files (see zone data files)
datasize options substatement, 78
date command, 189
date/time conversion, 189
ddns-domainname statement, 165, 166
ddns-rev-domainname statement, 165
debug (see troubleshooting)
default category (BIND 8), 184, 186
default records, returning, 84, 85
default-server options substatement, 203
default_syslog channel, 186, 187
delegation
    adding to zones, 83
    checking, 129–131
    domains, 8
    hidden primary masters, 139
    lame delegation checking, 111
    name servers, 133
    removing, 132
    reverse-mapping, 126, 127, 128, 129
    reverse-mapping zones, 83, 125, 126, 202
    subdomains, 124, 125
    Windows registration, 161
    zones, 7, 45

G

general category, 186
$GENERATE control statement
    adding records, 43
    record types, 43
    reverse-mapping, 127, 129
    server memory, 95
getopt( ) method, 102
Global Name Service (GNS), 58
glue fetching, 141
glue record (see A records)
GNS (Global Name Service), 58
group IDs, 49, 145
gTLDs, 6

H

h2n tool, 47
halt command (BIND 9), 20
hash values, 167
heartbeat intervals, 87
heartbeat-interval options substatement, 87
HELO SMTP commands, 93
HMAC-MD5 algorithm, 146
"Host" header (HTTP), 30
host tables, 47
host.conf file, 175
hosts
    adding, 26, 27
        with IPv6 interface, 201–202
        multihomed, 34
    migrating domain names, 123
    moving, 40, 41
    registration restrictions, 7
    sending syslog output to other, 187, 188
    storing location in zone data, 45, 46
HP-UX operating system, 173
HTTP "Host" header, 30

I

IANA (Internet Assigned Numbers
        Authority), 4
ICANN (Internet Corporation for Assigned
        Names and Numbers), 6
IETF, 199
IMAP mail servers, 44
IN (Internet) class
    default class, 27
    default view, 135
    for zones, 24
    queryperf and, 108
    update add command, 114
in-addr.arpa, 8, 165, 202

$INCLUDE control statement, 37, 43
include statement, 55, 56
incremental zone transfers (see IXFRs)
inet control channel, 49, 50, 156
inet controls substatement, 49, 203
Internet
    authoritative name server example, 18
    dedicated connectivity, 88
    hotel access services, 85
    IPv6 servers and, 200
    as resource, 2
Internet Assigned Numbers Authority (IANA), 4
Internet Corporation for Assigned Names
        and Numbers (ICANN), 6
Internet Software Consortium (see ISC)
IP addresses
    adding hosts, 26
    allow-query substatements, 150
    allow-transfer substatements, 148
    anti-spam tests, 93
    delegating reverse-mapping, 126, 128
    domain name registration, 7
    inet substatement argument, 50
    Internet access services, 85
    listen-on substatement and, 81
    looking up records with dig, 191
    mail servers and, 29
    mapping, 41, 43, 84
    masters substatement, 17, 120
    migrating domain names, 123
    multiple A records, 34
    name servers, 6
    preventing querying, 151
    returning answers dependent on, 69–70
    reverse-mapping with dig tool, 193, 194
    server command arguments, 116
    slave name servers, 73
    URLs, 30
    web servers, 29, 31
    zone statement component, 17
    zone transfers, 148
IPv6
    adding hosts with, 201–202
    listening for queries, 199, 200
    rndc and, 203
    sending queries from, 200, 201
    specifying, 200
Irix operating system, 173
ISC (Internet Software Consortium)
    BIND vulnerabilities, 10
    deprecating BIND 4, 158
    DHCP server, 166
    web site for, 2

root name servers *(continued)*
    root hints file, 15, 35
    setting up, 83, 84
    unnecessary queries, 29
root zone, 83, 84, 130
round robin, 31, 72, 172
routers, 152
rrset-order options substatement, 71
rsync program, 120

S

SAns (sent answers), 106
scp program, 120
search directive (resolv.conf file), 170
security
    allow-update substatement, 61
    authoritative name servers, 141, 142
    BIND 8 and 9 improvements, 155
    BIND 8 inet control channels, 50
    caching name servers, 142, 143
    chroot( ) environment, 143, 144
    concealing name server version, 134–136
    configuring firewalls, 137–138
    hidden primary masters, 139, 140
    nsupdate command --y option, 118
    preventing responses, 151, 152
    restricting queries answered, 149–150
    running other than root, 144, 145
    securing zone transfers, 147–149
    spoofing attacks, 152
    stealth slaves, 140, 141
    system-level precautions, 134
security category, 160, 189
semicolon (;), 48, 165
send command (nsupdate), 117
sequence space arithmetic, 38
serial numbers
    expire value, 25
    incrementing, 98
    notifying changes, 63
    resetting, 37, 39
    retry values, 25
    RNAME field, 24
    sequence space arithmetic, 38
    SOA record format, 24
    stub zones, 67
    zone transfers, 100
server command, 115
server statement
    BIND 4 slaves, 157
    controlling multiple processes, 103
    IXFRs and, 79

Microsoft DNS Server slaves, 158
    preventing querying, 151
    purpose of, 53
    rndc.conf file, 103
SERVFAIL responses, 78
services
    between hosts, 45
    easy to find, 44–45
    Network Solutions, 7
    registrar pricing, 6
    resolver service order, 173
    slave name service, 58
    time synchronization, 147
set port command (nslookup), 82
shell scripts, 22
SIG records, 61, 158
SIGINT signal, 20
signing
    control messages, 53
    forwarding dynamic updates, 63
    programmatically with TSIG, 179, 180
sign_tsig method (Net::DNS), 179
SIGTERM signal, 20
size argument (file substatement), 190
slash (/), 50, 171
slave name servers
    BIND 4 accommodating, 157, 158
    check-names substatement, 55
    configuring, 17, 18, 57, 58, 133
    dynamic updates, 62
    finding offsite, 58, 59
    hidden primary masters, 139
    IXFRs, 79
    Microsoft DSN Server, 159
    with multiple views, 72–76
    named.conf files, 55
    not listing, 63
    NOTIFY messages, 38, 64
    promoting, 119, 120
    protecting from abuse, 59, 60
    running Microsoft DNS Server, 158, 159
    setting up backups, 118
    SOA records, 24
    stealth slaves, 64, 140, 141
    transferring zone data, 23
    transfers-in options substatement, 111
    zone transfers, 100, 147, 148
slave zones, 57, 68, 87
SMTP commands, 93
SMTP mail servers, 44
SOA records
    dynamic updates, 61, 62
    host tables, 47

whitespaces, 26
whois service, 4, 5, 8
wildcard domain names, 42, 85
wildcards, 71
Windows 2000 operating system
    default timeouts for resolvers, 173
    DNS Console, 159
    dynamic updates, 154, 161–162
    hidden primary masters, 139
    precompiled BIND 9.2.1, 15
    preventing updates from, 160, 161
    resolver configuration window, 169, 170, 171
    resolver service order, 175
Windows 95 operating system, 170, 174
Windows 98 operating system, 170, 174
Windows ME operating system, 174
Windows NT operating system, 159, 172, 175
Windows operating system, 161–162
Windows resolvers
    appending domain names, 171
    configuring, 169, 170
    HOSTS and LMHOSTS files, 175
    timeouts and, 173
Windows XP operating system
    dynamic updates, 154, 161–162
    precompiled BIND 9.2.1, 15
    preventing updates from, 160, 161
    resolver configuration window, 170
WINS records, 159
WINS-R records, 159
working directories
    chroot( ) environment, 143
    default file location, 56
    name servers, 16
    named.stats file, 106, 109
    naming zone data files, 24
    options statement, 15
    relative paths, 57
    space considerations, 16

X

X Windows, 22

Z

zone data
    adding aliases, 27, 28
    adding intrazone domain names, 32, 33
    adding mail destinations, 28, 29
    adding multihomed hosts, 34
    cached records, 97

    changing cautions, 98
    checking, 96
    detecting errors, 111
    domain names, 41, 43
    filtering host tables, 47
    hidden primary masters, 139
    making services easy to find, 44–45
    manual changes to zones, 39, 40
    modifying, 98, 99
    name servers, 132
    root hints file, 35
    round robins, 31, 32
    serial numbers, 37, 39
    single file and multiple zones, 35, 37
    storing host location, 45, 46
    URLs, 30, 31
    web servers, 29, 30
    zone data files, 23–26
zone data files
    adding hosts, 26, 27
    adding MX records, 92
    authorizing edits, 145
    backup name, 17
    BIND 8/9 format, 156
    cleaning up, 20
    corruption cautions, 121
    creating, 23–26
    creating zones programmatically, 121
    double quotes, 16
    editing manually, 39
    filtering host tables, 47
    IXFR log file, 80
    modifying data, 98
    multiple directories, 56, 57
    multiple zones, 35, 37
    named-checkzone program, 95
    naming conventions, 18
    resource records, 23
    responses dependent on address, 70
    reverse-mapping, 128, 129, 202
    serial numbers, 39
    server address, 132
    slave name servers, 120
    specifying in zone statement, 16
    subdomains, 124
    synchronizing, 120
    testing name server configuration, 95
    troubleshooting, 182, 183
    zone transfers, 100
zone statement
    adding multiple, 18
    adding or removing zones, 99
    allow-query substatement, 149

About the Author

Cricket Liu matriculated at the University of California's Berkeley campus, that great bastion of free speech, unencumbered Unix, and cheap pizza. He joined Hewlett-Packard after graduation and worked for HP for nine years.

Cricket began managing the *hp.com* zone after the Loma Prieta earthquake forcibly transferred the zone's management from HP Labs to HP's Corporate Offices (by cracking a sprinkler main and flooding Labs' computer room). Cricket was hostmaster@hp.com for over three years, and then joined HP's Professional Services Organization to co-found HP's Internet consulting program.

Cricket left HP in 1997 to form Acme Byte & Wire, a DNS consulting and training company, with his friend (and now co-author) Matt Larson. Network Solutions acquired Acme in June 2000, and later the same day merged with VeriSign. Cricket worked for a year as Director of DNS Product Management for VeriSign Global Registry Services.

In September 2001, Cricket joined Men & Mice, an Icelandic company specializing in DNS software and services. He is currently their Vice President of Research and Development.

Cricket, his wife, Paige, and their son, Walt, live in Colorado with two Siberian Huskies, Annie and Dakota. On warm weekend afternoons, you'll probably find them on the flying trapeze or wakeboarding behind Betty Blue.

Colophon

Our look is the result of reader comments, our own experimentation, and feedback from distribution channels. Distinctive covers complement our distinctive approach to technical topics, breathing personality and life into potentially dry subjects.

The animal on the cover of *DNS and BIND Cookbook* is an opossum. Opossums are solitary, nocturnal mammals. They can be found in forests, fields, marshes, and farmlands, living in hollow trees, old buildings, and the abandoned dens of other animals. Opossums have clawless opposable toes on their hind feet that they can use like thumbs to grasp and hold onto branches. They can also hang by their tails for short periods of time. Opossums are the only North American marsupial: their young are born partially developed, and then carried by the female in a pouch called a marsupium for seven to ten weeks. The North American opossum is called the Virginia opossum (*Didelphis virginiana*).

Opossums are not aggressive. The phrase "playing possum" comes from an involuntary behavior the opossum exhibits when frightened: it rolls over, closes its eyes, and lays still. As its heartbeat slows, the animal gives the appearance of death, causing many predators to lose interest. When the opossum recovers from its shock, it wakes up and walks away. Opossum predators include foxes, coyotes, owls, and cars.

Colleen Gorman was the production editor and the proofreader for *DNS and BIND Cookbook*. Linley Dolby and Jane Ellin provided quality control. Lucie Haskins wrote the index.

Ellie Volckhausen designed the cover of this book, based on a series design by Edie Freedman. The cover image is a 19th-century engraving from the Dover Pictorial Archive. Emma Colby produced the cover layout with QuarkXPress 4.1 using Adobe's ITC Garamond font.

David Futato designed the interior layout. This book was converted to FrameMaker 5.5.6 with a format conversion tool created by Erik Ray, Jason McIntosh, Neil Walls, and Mike Sierra that uses Perl and XML technologies. The text font is Linotype Birka; the heading font is Adobe Myriad Condensed; and the code font is Lucas-Font's TheSans Mono Condensed. This colophon was written by Colleen Gorman.